Integrated English

GATEWAYS

2

STUDENT BOOK

Irene
Frankel

Victoria
Kimbrough

Oxford University Press

Oxford University Press
198 Madison Avenue
New York, NY 10016 USA

Great Clarendon Street
Oxford OX2 6DP England

Oxford New York

Auckland Cape Town Dar es Salaam Hong Kong Karachi
Kuala Lumpur Madrid Melbourne Mexico City Nairobi
New Delhi Shanghai Taipei Toronto

With offices in

Argentina Austria Brazil Chile Czech Republic France Greece
Guatemala Hungary Italy Japan South Korea Poland Portugal
Singapore Switzerland Thailand Turkey Ukraine Vietnam

OXFORD is a trademark of Oxford University Press.

ISBN-13: 978-0-19-434614-6
ISBN-10: 0-19-434614-5

Library of Congress Cataloging-in-Publication Data

Frankel, Irene.
    Gateway 2: student book / Irene Frankel, Victoria Kimbrough.
    136 p. 28 cm.—(Integrated English)
    Victoria Kimbrough's name appears first on the earlier eds.
    ISBN 0-19-434614-5
    1. English language—Textbooks for foreign speakers. 2. English
language—Spoken English—Problems, exercises, etc. 3. Listening—
Problems, exercises, etc. I. Kimbrough, Victoria, 1943—   II. Title.
III. Series.
    PE1128.F6748   1998
    428.2′4—dc21   97-6453

Senior Editor: Jeffrey Krum
Editor: Terra Brockman
Art Director: Lynn Luchetti
Designer: Shelley Himmelstein
Computer Assistant: David A. Easter
Art Buyer: Alexendra Rockafellar
Picture Researcher: Clare Maxwell
Production Manager: Abram Hall

Printing (last digit): 19 18 17 16 15 14 13

Printed in China

Cover direction: Shelley Himmelstein

Cover design/Photo montage: R.S. Winter

Illustrations by Dan Brown/Artworks, NY, John Courtney, John Dyess,
Andy Lendway, Jeff Seaver, Bill Silvers, Carol L. Strebel

Handwriting and realia by Annie Bissett, Todd Cooper, Jim DeLapine,
Shelley Himmelstein, Claudia Kehrhahn, Karen Minot, Ken Mowry

Location and studio photography by Dennis Kitchen

*The publishers would like to thank the following for their permission to
reproduce photographs:* Bob Abraham/The Stock Market; Archive Photos;
Kunio Awaki/The Stock Market; David Ball/The Picture Cube; David
Ball/The Stock Market; Tom Bean/The Stock Market; Arthur Beck/Photo
Researchers, Inc.; Tibor Bognar/The Stock Market: Brown Brothers;
Alan Carruthers/Photo Researchers, Inc.; Aaron Chang/The Stock Market;
Claude Charlier/The Stock Market; Gary Chowanetz/The Stock Market;
Chromosohm/Sohm/Photo Researchers, Inc.; Comstock; Marco Cristofori/
The Stock Market; Tim Davis/Photo Researchers, Inc.; David De Lossy/
The Image Bank; Werner Dietrich/The Image Bank; Patrick Donnell/
Photo Researchers, Inc.; Julio Donoso/Sygma; Frank Driggs/Archive
Photos; Randy Duchaine/The Stock Market; Robert Essel/The Stock
Market; Grant V Faint/The Image Bank; David Frazier/The Stock Market;
David R. Frazier/Photo Researchers, Inc.; Henry George/Comstock;
Frederica Georgia/Photo Researchers, Inc.; Ned Gillette/The Stock Market;
Francois Gohier/Photo Researchers, Inc.; Michael Going/The Image
Bank; Dennis M. Gottlieb/The Stock Market; Graham/Sygma; Tim
Graham/Sygma; Sylvain Grandadam/Photo Researchers, Inc.; Spencer
Grant/Photo Researchers, Inc.; Jeff Greenberg/Photo Researchers, Inc.;
Chris Hamilton/The Stock Market; Craig Hammell/The Stock Market;
Hellerstein/The Stock Market; John Henly/The Stock Market; Ted
Horowitz/The Stock Market; Illustrated London News/Archive Photos;
Thomas Ives/The Stock Market; Andre Jenny/International Stock; Mark
A. Johns/The Stock Market; Paul Kennedy/The Stock Market; Keystone/
Sygma; Matthew Klein/Photo Researchers, Inc.; Laszlo Studio/The Stock
Market; Dave Lawrence/The Stock Market; P Le Segretain/Sygma; Bullaty
Lomeo/The Image Bank; Leduc/Monkmeyer Press; Renee Lynn/Photo
Researchers, Inc.; John Madere/The Stock Market; Riccardo Marcialis/
Photo Researchers, Inc.; Markova/The Stock Market; The Mark Shaw
Collection/Photo Researchers, Inc.; Tom & DeeAnn McCarthy/The
Stock Market; Will & Deni McIntyre/Photo Researchers, Inc.; Joe
McNally/Sygma/Mastrorillo/The Stock Market; H.P Merten/The Stock
Market; Michael Ochs Archive; Lawrence Migdale/Photo Researchers, Inc.;
Roy Morsch/The Stock Market; Mug Shots/The Stock Market; Russell
Munson/The Stock Market; Lance Nelson/The Stock Market; Joseph
Nettis/Photo Researchers, Inc.; Nancy Ney/The Stock Market;
J. Barry O'Rourke/The Stock Market; Gabe Palmer/The Stock Market;
Paramount/The Kobal Collection; Jose Pelaez/The Stock Market; M.
Philippot/Sygma; David Pollack/The Stock Market: Popperfoto/
Archive Photos; Alon Reininger/The Stock Market; Jon Reis/The Stock
Market; John Roberts/The Stock Market; Roy/Explorer/Photo Researchers,
Inc.; Baron Sakiya/The Stock Market; Pete Saloutos/The Stock
Market; D. Sansoni/Panos Pictures; Nancy Santullo/The Stock Market;
Chuck Savage/The Stock Market; Blair Seitz/Photo Researchers, Inc.;
C. Simonpietri/Sygma; Ariel Skelley/The Stock Market; Joe Sohm/
Photo Researchers, Inc.; Sotographs/Liaison International; David
Stoeklein/The Stock Market; The Stock Market; R. Michael Stuckey/
Comstock: A. Tannenbaum/Sygma; Joe Towers/The Stock Market;
Universal Studios/The Kobal Collection; Denis Valentine/The Stock
Market; Peter Vanderwarker/Stock Boston; Jack Vartoogian/Jack
Vartoogian; Franklin J. Viola/Comstock; Phillip Wallick/The Stock
Market; William Waterfall/The Stock Market; Andrew Wood/Photo
Researchers, Inc.; Mike Yamashita/Woodfin Camp; Zefa-Becker/The
Stock Market; Zimbel/Monkmeyer Press

The publishers would also like to thank the following for their help:

p.4   stapler Courtesy of ACCO, USA Inc.
p. 8   Wheel of Fortune
p. 12   Drawing by Mankoff; © 1979, The New Yorker Magazine, Inc.
pp. 38 & 39   McDonald's
p. 41   *Love Story* © Paramount; *Jaws* © 1997 by Universal Studios, Inc.,
         courtesy of MCA Publishing Rights, a Division of MCA Inc. All
         Rights Reserved.
p 4   *Having Our Say* courtesy of Kodansha and the Delany Sisters.
         Photo of Delany sisters courtesy of Brian Douglas
p. 43   Courtesy of the N.C. Division of Archives and History
p. 56   YOU ARE MY SUNSHINE by Jimmie Davis & Charles Mitchell.
         Copyright © 1940 by Peer International Corporation. Copyright
         renewed. International Copyright Secured. Used by permission.
p. 73   University of California and Golden Bears™, University of
         Florida Gators™, University of Iowa Hawkeyes®, University
         of New Mexico Lobos, University of Virginia Cavaliers™,
         University of Wisconsin Badgers®
p. 76   Courtesy of Dr. Rob Gilbert
p. 78   Waikiki Hilton
pp. 78, 125, & 128   © 1996 Hertz System, Inc. Hertz is a registered
         service mark and trademark of Hertz System, Inc.

ACKNOWLEDGMENTS

The authors and publisher would like to thank the following people for reviewing and/or piloting components of this series. Their comments and suggestions contributed to its development and helped shape its content.

Daniel Altamirano Alonso, CENLEX-IPN, Mexico City, Mexico

Kevin Bandy, Boston English Learners, Caracas, Venezuela

Rory Baskin, Shoin Junior College, Nagoya, Japan

Steve Blakesley, Miyazaki Women's Junior College, Miyazaki, Japan

Douglas Buckeridge, Athénée Français, Tokyo, Japan

Angela Buckingham, Tokyo Air College, Tokyo, Japan

Simone Loyos Cabral, CCBEU, Bragança Paulista, Brazil

Rigoberto Castillo, CAFAM, Bogotá, Colombia

Katie Chiba, Trident School of Languages, Nagoya, Japan

Vania Peres Coianiz, CEL-LEP, São Paulo, Brazil

Steve Cornwell, Osaka Jogakuin Junior College, Osaka, Japan

Katy Cox, Casa Thomas Jefferson, Brasilia, Brazil

Walkiria Darahem, ACBEU Ribeirão Preto, Brazil

Jacob de Ruiter, CELE-UAEM, Toluca, Mexico

Barbara Bangle de Villavicencio, CELE-UAEM, Toluca, Mexico

Raúl Dorantes, Universidad del Valle, Mexico City, Mexico

Rosa Erlichman, UCBEU, São Paulo, Brazil

Georoidin Farrell, Bunka Institute of Language, Tokyo, Japan

Barry Fingerhut, Bunka Institute of Language, Tokyo, Japan

Kate Ford, Muroran Shimizugaoka, Hokkaido, Japan

Alejandra Gallegos, Interlingua, Aguascalientes, Mexico

Lesley Garcia, Bunka Institute of Language, Tokyo, Japan

Christine Gascho, Bunka Institute of Language, Tokyo, Japan

Juan Manuel García Godoy, CENLEX-IPN, Mexico City, Mexico

Rowena Gill, Cosmopolitan Language Consultants, Kobe, Japan

Noni Goertzen, Pacific College, Nagoya, Japan

Peter Grey, Seishu Junior College, Sapporo, Japan

Michael Guest, Shizuoka University, Shizuoko City, Japan

Robert Hickling, Bunka Women's University, Tokyo, Japan

Shelby Hopkins, Niigata Prefectural Board of Education, Niigata, Japan

Alys Jackson, Trident School of Languages, Nagoya, Japan

Leslie Kanberg, Kanda Institute of Foreign Languages, Tokyo, Japan

Kevin Keane, Kyushu Sangyo University, Fukuoka, Japan

Gerald Kurlandski, University Sidi Mohamed Ben Abdellah, Fez, Morocco

Nancy H. Lake, CEL-LEP, São Paulo, Brazil

Ann Leonard, ITESM, Guadalajara, Mexico

Amy Rita Lewis, Sophia University, Tokyo, Japan

Hsiao-wei Liu, Hsin-pu Institute of Technology and Business, Taipei, Taiwan

Jean-Pierre Louvrier, IBEU-CE, Fortaleza, Brazil

Juliet Marlier, Universidad de Las Américas, Puebla, Mexico

Gabriela Martínez, CEMARC, Mexico City, Mexico

Jeanette McLean, Tokyo Denki University, Chiba, Japan

Amy McNeese, Osaka College of Foreign Languages, Osaka, Japan

Katia Maria Medici, CEL-LEP, São Paulo, Brazil

Joaquìn Meza, Escuela Nacional Preparatoria No. 7-UNAM, Mexico City, Mexico

Lisa A. Miller, Aichi Shukutoku Girls High School, Nagoya, Japan

Patrick Murray, Experiment in International Living, Quito, Ecuador

Mary Sisk Noguchi, Meijo University, Junior College Division, Nagoya, Japan

Marie Nolan, Yung-chi YMCA, Taipei, Taiwan

Sonia Ocampo, Universidad del Valle, Mexico City, Mexico

Adelaide P. Oliveria, Salvador, Brazil

Teresa Peralta, CELE-UNAM, Mexico City, Mexico

Jaime Porras, CAFAM, Bogotá, Colombia

Charles Randles, ELSI International, Taipei, Taiwan

Michelle Albuquerque Ribeiro, IBEU-CE, Fortaleza, Brazil

Carol Rinnert, Hiroshima University, Hiroshima, Japan

Liz Robertson, Tokyo Air College, Tokyo, Japan

Sergio Rodarte, CELE-UAEM, Toluca, Mexico

Flávia Romano, Associacão Alumni, São Paulo, Brazil

Josè Leandro Rossi, CCBEU, São Paulo, Brazil

Sergio Rodarte, CELE-UAEM, Toluca, Mexico

Nidia Sarkis, UCBEU, São Paulo, Brazil

Lynn Shanahan, Toho High School, Nagoya, Japan

Steven Snyder, Yamagata Johoku Girls' Senior High School, Yamagata, Japan

Luzia Leme Tartari, CCBEU, Bragança Paulista, Brazil

Claudia E. Terribile, CCBEU, Bragança Paulista, Brazil

Mary Timothy, ITESM, Guadalajara, Mexico

Pei-Shan Ting, Tahwa Junior College of Technology and Commerce, Hsinchu, Taiwan

Mika Toff, Aichi Shukutoku Junior College, Nagoya, Japan

Luz María Uranga, Universidad del Valle, Mexico City, Mexico

Patricia Verduzco, CENLEX-IPN, Mexico City, Mexico

Juli Williams, Sapporo Lutheran College, Sapporo, Japan

Junko Yamanaka, Trident School of Languages, Nagoya, Japan

The authors would also like to thank all the people at OUP who helped in the planning and development of this series: Roy Gilbert, Susan Lanzano, Jeff Krum, Jane Sturtevant, Chris Foley, Bev Curran, Karen Brock, Silvia Dones, Pat O'Neill, Tyrone Prescod, Tareth Mitch, Shelley Himmelstein, Paul Hahn, and Clare Maxwell. We would especially like to thank our editor, Terra Brockman, for her unselfish dedication and hard work and limitless support, both editorial and moral.

We would also like to acknowledge the people with whom we have worked and studied who have taught us so much: Larry Anger, Shirley Brod, Oscar Castro, John Fanselow, Marjorie Fuchs, Cliff Meyers, Jenny Rardin, and Earl Stevick.

Scope and Sequence

Listening and Pronunciation	Reading	Writing
Clarification Strategies *Excuse me? Could you repeat that?* *Could you speak more slowly?* *How do you say…? How do you spell…? etc.*	**Recycle Activities** Review basic vocabularay sets: number, letters, months, dates, objects, countries, etc.	
Listen to a game show for correct answers Listen to phone conversations and take messages **Pronunciation:** Linking	Read an article about "Wheel of Fortune" **Strategies:** Use background knowledge; get meaning from context	Write a game-show–style introduction for yourself **Strategy:** Use a model
Listen to people's descriptions of themselves on dating videos Listen to a radio program for top characteristics of the ideal man/woman **Pronunciation:** Syllable stress in words	Read a script for a dating video **Strategies:** Brainstorm; read for specific information	Write your own dating video script **Strategies:** Prewriting: fill in a form; use a model
Listen to directions and find places on a map **Pronunciation:** Sentence stress: /ə/ in the unstressed words *and, at, or, the, to*	Read an invitation and directions to a party **Strategies:** Activate background knowledge; make inferences; scan for specific information	Write an invitation and directions to a party **Strategies:** Use a model; peer feedback
Listen to a tour guide for number and kinds of rooms in Buckingham Palace **Pronunciation:** Intonation of statements vs. compliments	Read advertisements for homes **Strategies:** Infer; deduce	Write a letter about a new home **Strategies:** Prewriting: draw a floor plan; use a model
Conversation Management Strategies Clarify and confirm; repeat what you heard; ask for spelling	**Grammar Learning Strategies** • Review • Notice language patterns	
Listen to a conversation for description of places in a city Listen to a conversation for activities and days of the week **Pronunciation:** *was/wasn't* and *were/weren't*	Read a restaurant review **Strategies:** Scan for specific information; infer a general opinion	Write a review of your favorite restaurant **Strategies:** Prewriting: discuss ideas with a partner; use a model
Listen to a conversation for specific information about famous firsts Listen to conversations to find out what a person thought of a movie **Pronunciation:** Consonant clusters with /r/	Read a biography of the Delany sisters **Strategies:** Activate background knowledge; hypothesize; scan for specific information; infer	Write a short biography **Strategies:** Brainstorm; make a list; use a model
Listen to a radio report for the best place to do certain activities Listen to a conversation for weekend activities **Pronunciation:** Past tense *-ed* endings	Read a letter about a vacation **Strategies:** Use background knowledge; brainstorm; scan for specific information	Write a letter about a vacation **Strategies:** Prewriting: analyze how a letter is organized; take and use notes; use a model
Listen to a mini-biography of Amelia Earhart and match information to pictures **Pronunciation:** Reduced form of *Did you*	Read brief stories **Strategy:** Use background knowledge	Write a story **Strategies:** Prewriting: discuss your opinion; use a model
Conversation Management Strategy Encourage the speaker: Express interest and ask a question	**Grammar Learning Strategies** • Review • Classify	

Listening and Pronunciation	Reading	Writing
Listen to a conversation for items found in a hotel room Listen to a conversation about where things are in a hotel room **Pronunciation:** Stress in compound nouns	Read a message about hotel needs **Strategies:** Skim; infer	Write a detailed message about hotel needs **Strategies:** Use a model; get peer feedback
Listen to a conversation for activities Listen to a telephone conversation for activities people are doing **Pronunciation:** *uh-huh* vs. *uh-uh*	Read a newspaper story about a robbery **Strategies:** Predict; infer	Write a paragraph solving the robbery **Strategy:** Use pictures to prompt writing
Listen to a news report for number of students in different college majors Listen to conversations about who is doing what **Pronunciation:** Reduction of *are you* in *Wh-* questions	Read an article about ways to be a good language learner; read dictionary entries **Strategies:** Pre-reading: activate background knowledge; compare ideas; get meaning from context	Write a learning list **Strategies:** Prewriting: make a list; use a model
Listen to a radio ad about a Hawaiian vacation for leisure activities Listen to a conversation about vacations and answer information questions **Pronunciation:** Reduced form of *going to (gonna)* in informal speech	Read a travel brochure **Strategies:** Skim; infer	Write a letter about a vacation you're going to take **Strategy:** Use pictures and a brochure as writing resources

Conversation Management Strategy
Keep the conversation going: answer and add

Grammar Learning Strategies
• Review
• Keep a grammar journal

Listening and Pronunciation	Reading	Writing
Listen to a radio show about popular picnic foods Listen to conversations and match people with their life events **Pronunciation:** Deletion of initial sounds and reduction of vowels in *him, her,* and *them*	Read an article about New Year's traditions around the world **Strategies:** Activate background knowledge; get meaning from context	Write about holiday customs in your country **Strategies:** Use a model; peer feedback
Listen to conversations in which people give excuses **Pronunciation:** Reduced forms of *have to* and *has to;* linking in *have a* and *has a*	Read etiquette questions and answers on e-mail **Strategy:** Skim	Write an answer to an etiquette query **Strategies:** Use a model and your background knowledge
Listen to conversations about how people feel and why **Pronunciation:** Intonation and phrasing in sentences with *when* clauses	Read an article about the fear of flying **Strategies:** Make a hypothesis; choose a title; identify topic sentences	Write a letter giving advice about a phobia **Strategies:** Use a model; peer feedback
Listen to a conversation and identify predictions about the future **Pronunciation:** Reduction in contractions with *will*	Read an article about how we'll pay for things in 2050 **Strategies:** Brainstorm; get meaning from context	Write your ideas about technology or travel in 2050 **Strategies:** Prewriting: discuss ideas; freewriting

Conversation Management Strategy
Use hesitaters

Grammar Learning Strategies
• Review
• Analyze your grammar errors

Introduction

Integrated English

Gateways is part of *Integrated English,* a flexible, six-level program for students of American English from beginner to intermediate level. The program is comprised of *Gateways, Transitions,* and *Explorations,* and has been designed for use either as three two-book courses or as a single, six-level program.

Gateways

Gateways is a two-level course for beginning-level adult and young adult learners of American English. *Gateways 2* is designed for students who have completed *Gateways 1,* and as an entry point for false beginners. It systematically builds upon what students already know and provides frequent recycling of basic vocabulary, grammar, and conversation management strategies, thereby allowing beginners to feel successful and gain confidence. *Gateways 2* uses meaningful adult contexts to provide practice in all four skills with an emphasis on speaking and listening.

Components of Gateways

Student Book

The Student Book contains 16 units. Each unit contains three 2-page lessons: the first two lessons emphasize listening and speaking, the last one reading and writing. A Strategy Session review unit appears after every four units. It consolidates the vocabulary and grammar from the preceding units while presenting important learning strategies for students to use both in class and at home. Grammar Summaries, which can be used for in-class reference or at-home study, appear at the back of the Student Book.

Cassettes and CDs

All listening activities, conversations, and pronunciation exercises from the Student Book are recorded. This symbol 🔲 next to an exercise indicates that it is recorded.

Workbook

The Workbook contains a variety of stimulating exercises that consolidate the material presented in the Student Book. Workbook exercises can be used in class or done as homework.

Teacher's Book

The Teacher's Book contains step-by-step instructions for each Student Book exercise as well as a wide variety of in-class extras: recycling exercises, optional activities, and reproducible material. It also contains useful background information such as language and culture notes and phonetic transcriptions for all proper nouns.

Key Features and Benefits of Gateways

Gateways enables beginning students to become competent and confident speakers of English by providing the following:

A firm foundation in the basics

Every language student must begin with the basic words (vocabulary) and a way to put these words together (grammar). *Gateways* explicitly presents all productive vocabulary, both visually and aurally. It also features a strong grammar syllabus, which highlights essential structures in clear, learner-friendly paradigms. The combination of a strong grammatical syllabus and explicit, incremental teaching of vocabulary gives beginning students the solid grounding they need. This firm foundation in the basics is further reinforced by task-based speaking, listening, reading, and writing activities which reinforce the grammar and vocabulary of each lesson while providing students with important skills work.

Opportunities to personalize

Students learn best when they are personally involved in the content of a lesson and when they can relate what they are learning to their own lives. By integrating grammar, vocabulary, and skills work around relevant, engaging topics, *Gateways* allows students to personalize their language learning. In each lesson, structured, more controlled activities introduce new language and set the stage for freer, communicative exchanges in which students use what they have learned to talk about themselves.

Confidence in using English

Many beginners lack the confidence to "try out their English." To help build students' confidence, *Gateways* includes many activities designed for pairs or small groups. These activities allow students to be actively engaged in communication while letting them feel relaxed enough to take risks. When students are communicating with each other directly in a relaxed classroom activity, they can more quickly become confident, competent speakers of English.

Conversation management strategies

Native speakers of English use a range of conversation management strategies when they converse. *Gateways 2* reviews the clarification strategies found in *Gateways 1* and presents other important conversation management strategies such as hesitating, expressing interest, agreeing, disagreeing, and keeping the conversation going. These strategies are modeled in the conversations and then practiced in later activities.

Opportunities to develop a range of learning strategies

By applying language learning strategies, students can become more successful, self-directed learners and make the process of language learning more enjoyable. *Gateways* integrates a range of strategies into its syllabus. Strategies such as activating background knowledge, predicting, and making inferences appear in every unit. In addition, four Strategy Sessions concentrate students' attention on becoming better, more effective learners—both in class and on their own.

Exercise types in the Student Book

Each unit of *Gateways* contains a variety of exercises that present and practice new language and develop speaking, listening, reading, and writing skills.

Vocabulary

Illustrations and photographs show the meaning of each core vocabulary item while the recording lets students hear how each item is pronounced. Students always hear the new words before they are asked to use them in communicative activities.

Grammar

New grammar is presented in the Conversation and practiced in the activities that follow. It is highlighted in easy-to-understand paradigms that show students how the language works.

Conversation

The Conversations introduce new grammar in natural, realistic contexts. They also model functions and clarification strategies and serve as models for later personalization.

Pronunciation

These exercises present important elements of spoken conversational English, such as stress, rhythm, intonation, and reductions.

Listening

Listenings feature a wide range of realistic material—conversations, news reports, interviews, etc.—and contain a variety of task-based listening exercises that develop important listening skills such as predicting, listening for specific information, and listening for gist.

Information Exchange

These are pair activities in which students communicate information to each other in order to accomplish a shared task. The activities provide controlled practice with grammar, vocabulary, and functions in communicative settings.

Reading

Each unit of *Gateways* contains realistic, high-interest readings. The readings are introduced with a pre-reading activity and are accompanied by a series of interesting exercises that allow students to demonstrate their reading comprehension.

Writing

Writing tasks are authentic and personal, and include filling in forms and writing postcards, notes, and letters. Many ideas from the writing process have been incorporated into the writing exercises. In *Gateways*, the emphasis is on getting thoughts down on paper. Students begin with prewriting activities, such as talking to a partner, brainstorming, or using a model, so that writing is a collaborative effort that also involves speaking and listening.

World View

World View boxes provide interesting cross-cultural information which relates to the topic of the unit. A question at the end of the World View encourages students to compare an aspect of their own culture to the one highlighted in the World View box.

Strategy Sessions

The Strategy Sessions focus on listening strategies, vocabulary learning strategies, clarification strategies, and grammar learning strategies. While focusing on strategies, each Strategy Session also provides a thorough review of the new grammar and vocabulary from the four units that precede it.

Getting Started

USEFUL EXPRESSIONS

INTRODUCTIONS

Learn your classmates' names. Use any expressions on page 2 that you need.

SAY "HI"

How are you?	Fine, thanks.	How are you?
	Great.	And you?
How are you doing?	Pretty good.	How about you?
How's it going?	Not bad.	
	OK.	

1. Practice the conversation.

   Silvia: Hi, Peter. How are you?
   Peter: Fine, thanks. How are you?
   Silvia: Not bad.

Personalize

2. Say "hi" to your classmates. Choose different expressions from the box.
   From now on, say "hi" to your classmates before class starts.

Who knows?

LISTENING

1. *Pairs.* Answer as many questions as you can.

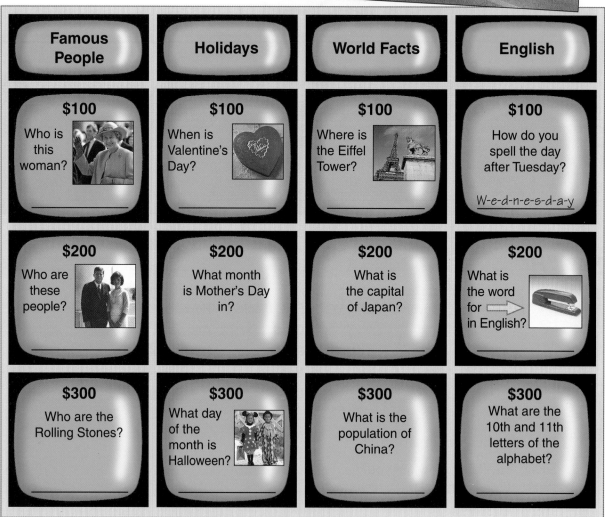

Famous People	**Holidays**	**World Facts**	**English**
$100 Who is this woman? _____	**$100** When is Valentine's Day? _____	**$100** Where is the Eiffel Tower? _____	**$100** How do you spell the day after Tuesday? W-e-d-n-e-s-d-a-y
$200 Who are these people? _____	**$200** What month is Mother's Day in? _____	**$200** What is the capital of Japan? _____	**$200** What is the word for ⇨ in English? _____
$300 Who are the Rolling Stones? _____	**$300** What day of the month is Halloween? _____	**$300** What is the population of China? _____	**$300** What are the 10th and 11th letters of the alphabet? _____

2. Listen to the game show and check your answers.

3. *Pairs.* Test your partner. Student A, ask Student B five of the questions. Student B, close your book and answer. Then switch roles.

Ⓐ When is Valentine's Day?
Ⓑ February 14.

GRAMMAR

Where	is	Pelé from?	He	's	from Brazil.
When		New Year's Day in Mexico?	It		January 1.
Who	are	the New York Yankees?	They	're	a baseball team.
What		the articles in English?			*a, an,* and *the.*

YOUR OWN GAME SHOW

1. *Pairs.* Use one book. Write three questions for each category. Use *Who, What, When,* and *Where* and the verb *to be.* Be sure you know the answers!

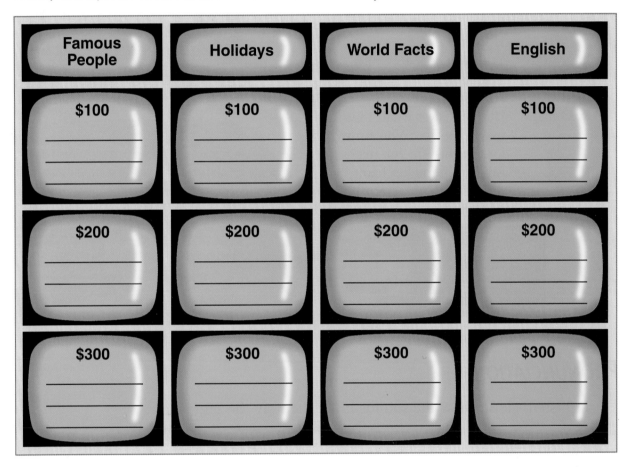

Famous People	Holidays	World Facts	English
$100	$100	$100	$100
$200	$200	$200	$200
$300	$300	$300	$300

2. *Two pairs.* Play the game show.

   - Pair 1, stay here.
   - Pair 2, go to page 116.
   - Pair 1, listen to the category and amount Pair 2 chooses. For example, *Holidays for $100.*
   - Ask Pair 2 your question. For example, *What month is Father's Day in?*
   - Tell Pair 2 if their answer is correct or incorrect. If Pair 2 is correct, they get the money.
   - Continue playing until Pair 1 has asked all 12 questions.
   - Then go to page 116. Switch roles and play the game again.
   - The pair with the most money wins.

GRAMMAR

Is	Joe	there?		he	is.		he	isn't.
	Sue			she			she	
			Yes,	I	am.	No,	I	'm not.
Are	you	free?						
	they			they	are.		they	aren't.

CONVERSATION

 Practice the conversation.

Joe's Brother: Hello?

Roxanne: Hello. This is **Roxanne**. Is **Joe** there?

Joe's Brother: Yes, **he** is. Just a minute.

Roxanne: Thanks.

Joe: Hi, **Roxanne**.

Roxanne: Hi, **Joe**. Guess what! I just got two tickets to "**Who Knows?**" for tonight. Are you free?

Joe: Am I free? You bet I am!

PRONUNCIATION

 1. Listen. Notice how the sounds link. Then say the sentences.

Yes, I (y) am. No, (w) I'm not.

Yes, he (y) is. No, (w) he (y) isn't.

Yes, they (y) are. No, they (y) aren't.

2. Now say these sentences.

Yes, she (y) is. No, she (y) isn't.

Yes, it is. No, (w) it isn't.

Personalize

3. *Groups of three.* Practice the conversation again. Use your own information. (You can have tickets to any event.)

LISTENING

📼 1. Listen to the conversation and fill in the blanks.

Mr. Moore: Hello?

Cheryl: Hello. This is Cheryl Donahue. <u>Is Joe there</u>?

Mr. Moore: _____ sorry. _____. Can _____ take a message?

Cheryl: Yes. Please tell him to call me tonight or tomorrow.

_____ 942-0865.

Mr. Moore: 942-0865?

Cheryl: _____.

Mr. Moore: And _____, please?

Cheryl: Donahue. D-O-N-A-H-U-E.

Mr. Moore: _____. I'll give him the message.

Cheryl: _____.

JOE,
CALL CHERYL DONAHUE
TONIGHT OR TOMORROW.
HER PHONE NUMBER
IS 942-0865.
DAD

2. *Pairs.* Check your answers. Practice the conversation.

📼 3. Listen to the conversations and take the messages.

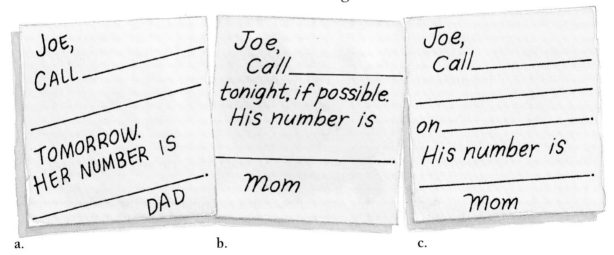

a.   b.   c.

4. *Pairs.* Check your answers.

Ⓐ What's the first message?
Ⓑ Call Marcia Greenbaum tomorrow. Her number is…

ROLE PLAY

Pairs. Student A, call Joe. Student B, take a message.
Student B, call Roxanne. Student A, take a message.

READING AND WRITING

1. Look at the picture. What kind of show is "Wheel of Fortune"? What do you know about this show?

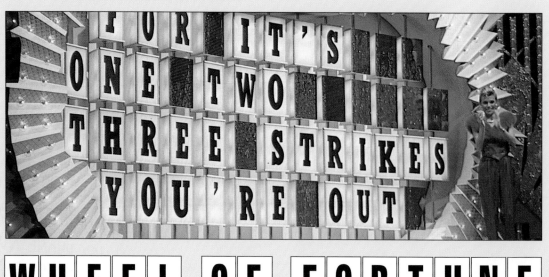

WHEEL OF FORTUNE
FAST FACTS

▶ "Wheel of Fortune" started on daytime television in the United States in 1975.

▶ It's the most popular TV game show in the world.

▶ 100 million people in 52 countries watch "Wheel of Fortune" every week.

▶ More than 10,000 people a year try out for the show; 1,500 people become contestants.

▶ "Wheel of Fortune" gives away about $6 million in cash and prizes a year, an average of $45,000 per show.

▶ Deborah Cohen and Peter Argyropoulis of Los Angeles are the biggest winners to date. They won $146,529 in cash and prizes!

2. Vocabulary in context. *Pairs.* Read the article and label the pictures. Use these words: *cash, contestants, prizes, winner.*

a. _____   b. _____   c. _____   d. _____

3. Read the article again. Which fact is the most interesting to you?

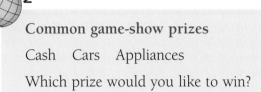

Common game-show prizes

Cash   Cars   Appliances

Which prize would you like to win?

4. The contestants on "Who Knows?" introduced themselves. Here's what they said.

My name is Elena Morales. I'm from Mexico City, and I'm a lawyer. I'm married and I have two beautiful children, Eduardo, 12 and Ana, 10. In my free time I like to play tennis and go to the movies.

My name is Kenji Suzuki. I'm an English teacher, and I teach in a large high school. I live in Osaka with my wife and son, Ichiro. I'm a big baseball fan, and I love to play golf.

My name is Wilma Spano. I'm from Rio de Janeiro, and I'm a model. I work for a large international modeling agency. I'm single, but I have a very nice boyfriend, Roger. I like to go dancing, and, of course, I love to go to the beach.

5. Imagine that you're going to be a contestant on a game show. On a separate piece of paper, write an introduction for yourself.

6. *Pairs.* Share your introductions.

What's she like?

VOCABULARY

1. Listen to the people in the dating service videos. Put a check (✓) next to all the adjectives that describe the person.

Donna   ✓ beautiful   ___ shy   ✓ adventurous   ___ rich

Mike   ___ intelligent   ___ good-looking   ___ charming   ___ generous

Will   ___ romantic   ___ kind   ___ friendly   ___ hardworking

Lynn   ___ ambitious   ___ fun to be with   ___ attractive   ___ honest

GRAMMAR

I'm		I	'm	not	
He's	intelligent.	He	is	n't	rich.
She's		She			

2. *Pairs.* Check your answers.

   Ⓐ Donna is beautiful and adventurous, but she isn't shy and she isn't rich.
   Ⓑ Right. Mike is…

PRONUNCIATION

1. Listen. Notice the stressed syllable in each word.

   ●   ●   ●

beautiful   adventurous   intelligent

2. Listen and mark the stressed syllable in each word. Then say the words.

charming   romantic   attractive   honest   ambitious   friendly

LISTENING

1. What's the ideal woman like? What's the ideal man like? Listen to the radio news program and number the adjectives in the correct order.

Ideal woman:	__ beautiful	__ intelligent	__ fun to be with	__ kind	__ sexy
Ideal man:	__ good-looking	__ ambitious	__ intelligent	__ rich	__ kind

2. *Pairs.* Check your answers.

   Ⓐ According to men, the ideal woman is first, kind; second,….
   Ⓑ Right. And according to women, the ideal man is….

TAKE A SURVEY

1. What are the three most important things to you in an ideal mate? Write three adjectives: _____ _____ _____

2. On a separate piece of paper, make a chart like this:

Qualities	Men	Women
intelligent		
fun to be with		
adventurous		
_____		
_____		

3. Survey at least ten people. Tally the responses.

   Ⓐ My ideal mate is intelligent, fun to be with, and adventurous. What about yours?
   Ⓑ Mine is…

4. Report to the class. For example, *According to my survey, the ideal woman is first,….*

VOCABULARY

1. Listen to the people in the dating service videos. Find the ideal mate for each person. Write *Donna*, *Mike*, *Will*, or *Lynn* under the picture of their ideal mate.

tall	average height	short	slim	medium build	heavy
_____	_____	Donna	_____	_____	_____

curly hair	blond hair	dark hair	short hair	long hair	straight hair
_____	_____	_____	_____	_____	_____

2. *Pairs.* Check your answers.

Ⓐ Donna's ideal mate is short and slim. He has dark hair and blue eyes.

Ⓑ Right. And Mike's ideal mate is…

BINGO

Go to page 117.

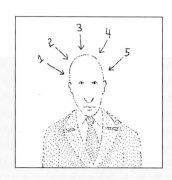

Five Major Warning Signs of Baldness

Do	you	wear glasses?	Yes,	I	do.	No,	I	don't.	I	wear	contact lenses.
Does	he			he	does.		he	doesn't.	He	wears	

CONVERSATION

1. Practice the conversation.

Sandy: Hello?

Joe: Hello. Is **Dan Martin** there?

Sandy: **Dan Martin?** I don't know. What does he look like?

Joe: Well, he's **tall** and **slim**, and he has **long blond** hair.

Sandy: **Tall** and **slim** with **long blond** hair. Does he wear glasses?

Joe: **No, but he has a beard and mustache and...**

Sandy: Oh, OK. I see him. Hold on, please.

2. *Pairs*. Practice the conversation again. Ask for Sam, Alan, and Jesse.

MAKE IT PERSONAL

1. *Pairs*. Describe your best friend or someone in your family. For example, *My best friend's name is Natalie. She's intelligent, kind, fun to be with, and honest. She's short and slim and she has straight black hair and brown eyes. I think she's really pretty.*

2. *Pairs*. Describe your boyfriend, girlfriend, husband, wife, or ideal mate. For example, *My ideal mate is beautiful, sexy, rich, intelligent, fun to be with, honest, and adventurous. She's....*

READING AND WRITING

1. *Pairs.* Brainstorm. Look at the picture of Donna. Cover her dating video script below. What do you remember about Donna and her ideal mate? Make a list, for example:

DONNA	DONNA'S IDEAL MATE
She's beautiful.	He's short.

2. Read Donna's script for her dating video.
   How many things did you remember correctly?

"Hi. I'm Donna. I think I'm beautiful, and I know I'm sexy. I'm adventurous, and let's see...I love to go out and talk to people—I'm not at all shy. I'm not rich either—not yet. But some day, I hope I will be."

"I'm a very active person. On weekends, I like to go rollerblading and skydiving. At night, I like to eat out, go dancing, and go to parties."

"My ideal mate is fun to be with and adventurous, too. He's intelligent, kind, and charming. He may not be rich, but he's hardworking and ambitious."

"What do I want my ideal man to look like? Well, I really like short men. So my ideal man is short and slim, and he has blue eyes. I love blue eyes. And I like dark hair—brown or black and a little long."

3. Read Donna's script again. Fill in her video dating form.

GETTING TOGETHER VIDEO DATING SERVICE

a. **Name:** _Donna DeMilo_

b. **Circle the adjectives that describe you best.**
Personality (adventurous,) ambitious, charming, friendly, fun to be with, hardworking, honest, intelligent, kind, romantic, sexy
Physical **Build:** tall, average height, short, slim, medium build, heavy
Hair: long, short, straight, <u>curly</u>, blond, black, brown, red
Other: good-looking, (beautiful,) pretty, attractive

c. **What do you like to do in your free time?**
On weekends I like to go rollerblading and skydiving.
At night I like to eat out, go dancing, and go to parties.

d. **Circle the most important characteristics of your ideal mate.**
Personality adventurous, ambitious, charming, friendly, fun to be with, hardworking, honest, intelligent, kind, romantic, sexy
Physical **Build:** tall, average height, short, slim, medium build, heavy
Hair: long, short, straight, curly, blond, black, brown, red
Other: good-looking, beautiful, pretty, attractive

4. Complete this video dating form for yourself.

GETTING TOGETHER VIDEO DATING SERVICE

a. **Name:** _____

b. **Circle the adjectives that describe you best.**
Personality adventurous, ambitious, charming, friendly, fun to be with, hardworking, honest, intelligent, kind, romantic, sexy
Physical **Build:** tall, average height, short, slim, medium build, heavy
Hair: long, short, straight, curly, blond, black, brown, red
Other: good-looking, beautiful, pretty, attractive

c. **What do you like to do in your free time?**
_____

_____

d. **Circle the most important characteristics of your ideal mate.**
Personality adventurous, ambitious, charming, friendly, fun to be with, hardworking, honest, intelligent, kind, romantic, sexy
Physical **Build:** tall, average height, short, slim, medium build, heavy
Hair: long, short, straight, curly, blond, black, brown, red
Other: good-looking, beautiful, pretty, attractive

5. You are going to make a dating video like Donna's. Write your dating video script.

6. *Pairs.* Share your video script.

How do I get to the White House?

LISTENING

1. Listen to the conversations. Write the letter of the place on the map.   *museum of American*

a. the White House

b. the Washington Monument

c. the Lincoln Memorial

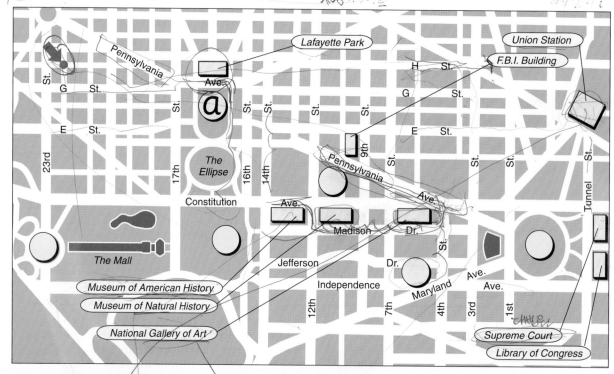

d. the Capitol Building

e. the Old Post Office

f. the Air and Space Museum

2. *Pairs.* Check your answers.

Ⓐ Where's the White House?
Ⓑ It's right here.

GRAMMAR

Walk	along H street. 걸어서		**walk**	along G Street. 가 즐길	숙제
Go	two blocks. 블이나	**Don't**	**go**	three blocks. 세 블럭 가지마 얼른	
Turn	right. 어떻게 둘아		**turn**	left.	

CONVERSATION

 1. Practice the conversation.

Woman: Excuse me. How do I get to the White House?

Man: Walk along H Street to Pennsylvania Avenue. Turn right and go about three blocks.

Woman: OK. Just a second. I go to Pennsylvania Avenue. And then I turn left and then…

Man: No. Don't turn left. Turn right and walk about three blocks. You can't miss it.

Woman: OK, thanks. 무슨 내용?

Man: You're welcome.

E-Bay (인터넷)
찾았더니 애기해줬다. 얼마, 얼마

2. *Pairs.* Practice the conversation again. Use other places of interest on the map.

ROLE PLAY

Pairs. Student A, you're from out of town. Ask Student B for directions to places near your school. For example:

Ⓐ Excuse me. How do I get to the post office?
Ⓑ Walk along…

GRAMMAR		
How		get to the White House?
Where	**do I**	transfer?
Which train		take?

CONVERSATION

Practice the conversation.

Man: Excuse me. Does this train go to **National Airport?**

Woman: No, it doesn't. You have to take this train to **Gallery Place** and then transfer to the **yellow** line and…

Man: Wait. I'm sorry. Where do I transfer?

Woman: At **Gallery Place.**

Man: **Gallery Place.** And then which train do I take?

Woman: Take the **yellow** line and get off at the **National Airport** station.

Man: OK. The **yellow** line. How many stops is it?

Woman: Hmmm … I'm not sure … **five** or **six**.

Subway Stops for Popular Attractions

Capitol South
• Capitol Building
• Library of Congress

Federal Center Southwest
• Department of Education
• Air and Space Museum

Smithsonian
• Washington Monument
• National Museum of American History

Federal Triangle
• The Old Post Office
• F.B.I. Building

Metro Center
• The White House
• The National Portrait Gallery

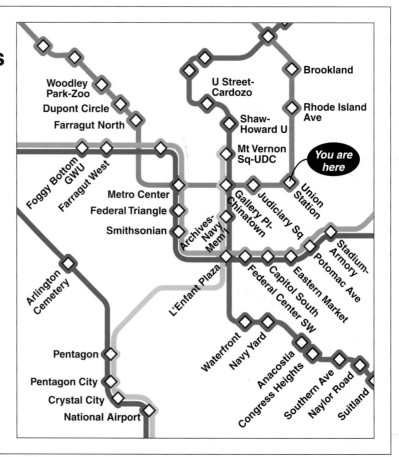

PRONUNCIATION

1. Listen. Notice that vowels in unstressed words such as *and, at, or, the,* and *to* are often reduced to /ə/. Then listen and repeat.

Go to K Street and turn left.
How do I get to the White House?

Get off at the Gallery Place station.
It's five or six stops.

2. Listen to these sentences and fill in the blanks with *and, at, or, the,* or *to.* Then say the sentences.

   a. Does this train go _____ National Airport?

   b. Do I turn left _____ right?

   c. You have _____ take _____ red line _____ Union Station.

   d. Transfer _____ _____ blue line _____ Metro Center _____ go two stops.

3. *Pairs.* Take turns asking and giving directions. Use the conversation and subway map on page 18.

You are at	You want to go to
Dupont Circle	
Waterfront	
Union Station	
Brookland	

MAKE IT PERSONAL

1. *Pairs.* Student A, you're having a party after class. Give Student B directions to the party. For example, *Take the Number 7 bus and get off at 14th Street. Walk along 14th Street for two blocks to Fifth Avenue. Turn right and go a block and a half. My apartment is on Fifth Avenue between 12th and 13th Streets.*

2. Report to the class. For example, *To get to Michael's party, I take....*

READING AND WRITING

WORLD VIEW

Loan words

English has many "loan words," words that come from other languages. RSVP is from the French phrase that means "please respond."

What are some loan words in your language?

1. Look at the invitation and directions. What are they for?

   a. a business meeting   **b.** a wedding   **c.** a party

You're Invited!

Who: Rebecca and Andy Weiss
Where: 225 Holland Avenue
Rome, New York
When: Saturday, September 28
8:00 p.m.
RSVP: (315) 555-3181 by September 21

DIRECTIONS

Take Route 4 to the River Road exit. Turn left at the light (River Road). Stay on River Road for about 2 miles to Holland Avenue. Turn left. Our house is the third house on the right.

2. You plan to attend. What should you do by September 21?

   a. Call Rebecca and Andy.
   b. Write to Rebecca and Andy.
   c. Buy a present for Rebecca and Andy.

3. Look at the map. Where is Rebecca and Andy's house? Put an X on the map.

4. Imagine that you're going to have a party. Write an invitation.

You're Invited!

Who: _____

Where: _____

_____

When: _____

_____

RSVP: _____

5. On a separate piece of paper, write directions to your party. Draw a map, but don't show where the party is.

6. *Pairs.* Give your directions and map to your partner. Read your partner's directions and find the party on his or her map.

How many bedrooms are there?

VOCABULARY

1. Listen to the tour guide at Buckingham Palace. Fill in the blanks with the number you hear. Add an *s* to the word if you need to make it plural.

   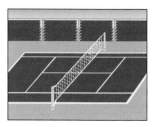

<u>240</u> bedroom <u>s</u>   _____ bathroom__   _____ office__   _____ tennis court__

   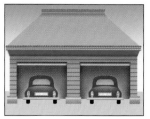

_____ gym__   _____ garden__   _____ art gallery__   _____ garage__

GRAMMAR				
How many bedrooms **are there?**	**There**	**'s**	one	(bedroom).
		are	two	(bedrooms).
		aren't	any	

2. *Pairs.* Check your answers.

   (A) How many bedrooms are there?
   (B) There are 240 bedrooms.

CONVERSATION

1. Practice the conversation.

Ellen: Hi, Pete. How's the new apartment?

Pete: Great! It has everything!

Ellen: Oh, yeah? Like what?

Pete: Well, there's **a living room, a dining room, and a kitchen.** Then there are **two bedrooms and two bathrooms.** And there are lots of windows, so it's very sunny.

Ellen: Sounds great. Is there a garage?

Pete: Uh-huh. There's a pool, too. And a balcony.

Ellen: Wow! When can I visit?

2. Which one is Pete's new apartment?

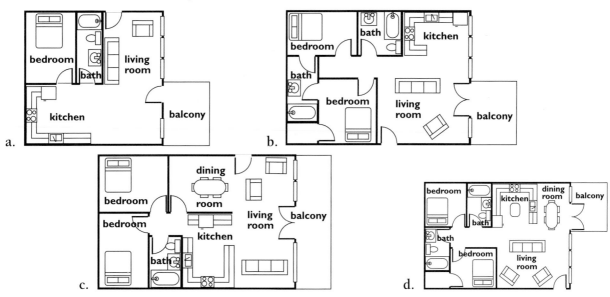

a.

b.

c.

d.

3. *Pairs.* Practice the conversation again. Use the other apartments.

ROLE PLAY

1. *Pairs.* Student A, you've just won the lottery. Student B, you're an architect. Student A, describe your ideal house. Student B, ask questions and take notes. For example, *My ideal house is very big. There are five bedrooms, four bathrooms...*

2. Report to the class about your partner's ideal house. For example, *Joan's ideal house is very big. There are....*

VOCABULARY

1. Match the words and the pictures.

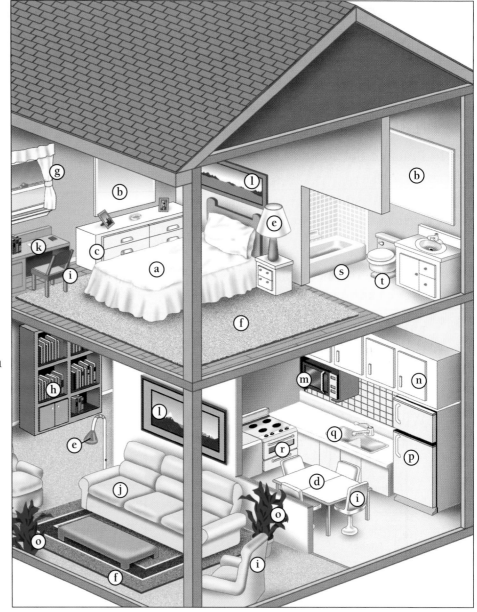

_S_ bathtub

____ bed

____ bookcase

____ cabinet

____ chair

____ couch

____ curtains

____ desk

____ dresser

____ lamp

____ microwave oven

____ mirror

____ picture

____ plants

____ refrigerator

____ rug

____ sink

____ stove

____ table

____ toilet

2. Listen and check your answers.

Who knows?

INFORMATION EXCHANGE

Whose is whose?

Pairs.
Student A, go to page 119.
Student B, go to page 120.

CONVERSATION

Practice the conversation.

Paul: Who is it?
Sharon: It's me … **Sharon.**
Paul: Oh, hi. Come in.
Sharon: What a nice apartment!
Paul: Thank you.
Sharon: **That's a beautiful couch! And what a great lamp!**
Paul: Thanks. Actually, this is my favorite room.
Sharon: I can see why.

PRONUNCIATION

1. Listen. Notice the difference in tone between the statements and compliments.

Statement	Compliment
That's a beautiful couch.	That's a beautiful couch!
Those are great chairs.	Those are great chairs!
That's a nice picture.	That's a nice picture!

2. Listen. Put a period (.) for statements and an exclamation point (!) for compliments.

What a nice desk   Those are beautiful pictures
Those are nice curtains   That's a great table
That's a beautiful plant   That's a pretty rug
What a sunny room   What a great lamp

3. Say the sentences in Exercise 2 that have exclamation points.

Monthly rents for 3-bedroom apartments in prime locations:

Hong Kong	$9,514	London	$3,813
Tokyo	$8,490	Mexico City	$3,700
São Paulo	$5,000	Milan	$2,812
Manhattan	$4,000	Frankfurt	$2,840

What is the average monthly rent in your city?

ROLE PLAY

Pairs. Look at the pictures on page 131. Choose your favorite room and show it to your partner. Role-play a conversation like the one between Paul and Sharon.

READING AND WRITING

1. Look at the ads and the floor plans. Write the words for each abbreviation.

FR _____   Kit _____

LR _____   Bth _____

DR _____   BR _____

BEAUTIFUL VICTORIAN HOME

Park Ridge. $275,000. Elegant Victorian house with large porch and balcony. 4BRs, 2.5 Bths, large LR, and formal DR. Huge FR with fireplace. Call 919-563-1128.

ROOMY RANCH HOME

Greenville. $185,000. Spacious ranch house with large sunny LR, beautiful eat-in kit, 3 BRs, 1.5 Bths, 2-car garage, and central A/C. Call 919-293-0264.

TUDOR-STYLE HOME

Oakland. $209,000. Charming 2-story Tudor house at a great price. 3BRs, 1.5 Bths, FR, LR with fireplace, and large new kit. Quiet street near park, lots of trees. Call 919-923-3958.

COZY CAPE-COD HOME

Whitestone. $149,000. A warm, inviting home in lovely neighborhood. 2BRs, 1.5 Bths, modern kit, large formal DR, sunny LR. Call 919-743-0438.

2. You want to buy a house. It must have at least three bedrooms, two bathrooms, and a sunny living room. Scan the ads. Check (✓) the houses you want to see.

3. Match the floor plans to the houses in Exercise 1. Write the locations.

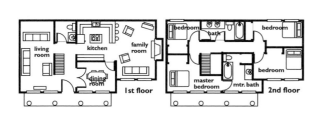
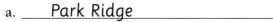

a. ___Park Ridge___

b. _____

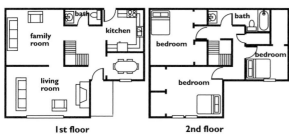

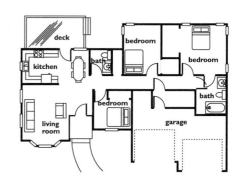

c. _____

d. _____

4. *Pairs.* Discuss. Which house is your favorite? Why? For example, *I like the house in Park Ridge because...*

5. Imagine that you have just moved into your ideal house. Draw a floor plan on a separate piece of paper.

6. Write a letter to a friend about your new house. For example,

> June 12
>
> Dear Pat,
>   Hi! Well, we're finally in our new house. It's beautiful!
>   There's a huge living room, with lots of windows and wall-to-wall carpeting. The walls are light blue with dark blue

7. *Pairs.* Share your letters.

LISTENING

Strategy: Activating background knowledge

1. Look at the picture. You're going to hear a conversation. Write five words you think you will hear.

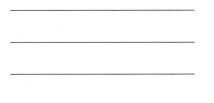

_____

_____

_____

_____

_____

2. Listen to the conversation. Were your predictions correct?

Strategy: Listening for specific information

3. Listen to the conversation again. Answer these questions:

  a. How many bedrooms are there? _____

  b. How many bathrooms are there? _____

  c. What other rooms are there? _____

  _____

  d. Is there a balcony? _____

  e. Is there a nice view? _____

  f. How much is the apartment? _____

4. *Pairs.* Check your answers.

  (A) There are three bedrooms.
  (B) Right. And....

VOCABULARY LEARNING

Strategy: Identifying words that are similar in your language

For example: English–intelligent
Portuguese–inteligente
Spanish–inteligente

1. Which of these words are similar to words in your language? Write the words in your language. Then check your answers with a partner's.

airport   party
capital   romantic
office   charming
popular   garden
train   television

2. Look through Units 1–4. Find ten words that are similar to words in your language. Write the English words and the words in your language. Then check your answers with a partner's.

Strategy: Making categories

For example: **Cities**   **Countries**
Paris   France
Sydney   Australia

1. Put these words into two categories. Use a separate piece of paper.

adventurous   heavy
average height   honest
bald   intelligent
beautiful   kind
friendly   slim
good-looking   tall

2. *Pairs.* Student A, show your categories to Student B. Are your categories the same?

3. Look at the vocabulary in Unit 4 on pages 22 and 24. Put the words into two or more categories. Then show your categories to a partner.

CONVERSATION MANAGEMENT

Strategies: Clarifying and confirming

1. *Pairs.* Here are two conversations. Cover your partner's side of the page. Say the two conversations. Student A, begin.

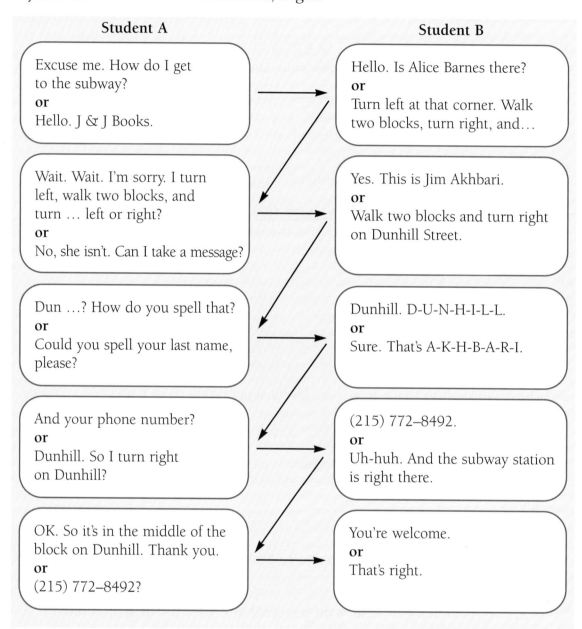

Student A

Excuse me. How do I get to the subway?
or
Hello. J & J Books.

Wait. Wait. I'm sorry. I turn left, walk two blocks, and turn ... left or right?
or
No, she isn't. Can I take a message?

Dun ...? How do you spell that?
or
Could you spell your last name, please?

And your phone number?
or
Dunhill. So I turn right on Dunhill?

OK. So it's in the middle of the block on Dunhill. Thank you.
or
(215) 772–8492?

Student B

Hello. Is Alice Barnes there?
or
Turn left at that corner. Walk two blocks, turn right, and…

Yes. This is Jim Akhbari.
or
Walk two blocks and turn right on Dunhill Street.

Dunhill. D-U-N-H-I-L-L.
or
Sure. That's A-K-H-B-A-R-I.

(215) 772–8492.
or
Uh-huh. And the subway station is right there.

You're welcome.
or
That's right.

2. Underline all the clarification and confirmation strategies in Exercise 1. (Hint: There are six.)

3. *Pairs.* Role-play. Student A, ask Student B for directions. Take notes. Use any of the clarification or confirmation strategies in Exercise 1.

4. *Pairs.* Role-play. Student A, call Student B and ask for Ken Wada. Ken isn't there. Student B, take a message. Use any of the clarification or confirmation strategies in Exercise 1.

GRAMMAR LEARNING
Strategy: Reviewing

Pairs. Use one book. Play *Strike It Rich!*

- Put your markers in the Start/Finish space.
- Player 1, flip a coin. Heads = 1; tails = 2. Move your marker one or two spaces.
- Read the question out loud. Give a true answer. Answer Yes/No questions with a short answer. If the answer is no, give the correct answer. For example, **Question: Is your teacher from Canada? Answer: No, she isn't. She's from the United States.**
- If your answer is wrong, move back to the space you were on. If your answer is correct, stay on the space. Write down the amount of money you won.
- Player 2, take your turn.
- The player with the most money at the Finish is the winner.

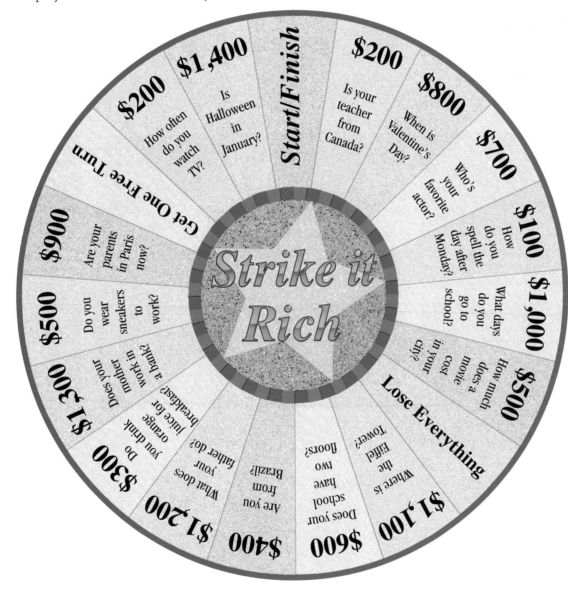

Strike it Rich

- **Start/Finish**
- $200 — Is your teacher from Canada?
- $800 — When is Valentine's Day?
- $700 — Who's your favorite actor?
- $100 — How do you spell the day after Monday?
- $1,000 — What days do you go to school?
- $500 — How much does a movie cost in your city?
- Lose Everything
- $1,100 — Where is the Eiffel Tower?
- $600 — Does your school have two floors?
- $400 — Are you from Brazil?
- $1,200 — What does your father do?
- $300 — Do you drink orange juice for breakfast?
- $1,300 — Does your mother work in a bank?
- $500 — Do you wear sneakers to work?
- $900 — Are your parents in Paris now?
- Get One Free Turn
- $200 — How often do you watch TV?
- $1,400 — Is Halloween in January?

Strategy: Noticing language patterns   Go to page 121.

How was the trip?

VOCABULARY

1. Listen to the conversation between Alice and Ben. Check (✓) the pictures that match what you hear.

HOTEL

 ✓ nice   ___ awful

STREETS

___ quiet   ___ noisy

FOOD

___ delicious   ___ horrible

RESTAURANTS

___ expensive   ___ inexpensive

WEATHER

___ beautiful   ___ terrible

PEOPLE

___ friendly   ___ unfriendly

GRAMMAR

The hotel	**was**	nice.
The streets	**were**	noisy.

2. *Pairs.* Check your answers.

  Ⓐ The hotel was nice.
  Ⓑ Right. And the streets were….

CONVERSATION

🎙 Practice the conversation.

Alice: How was your trip? I just talked to Ben. He said it was really nice.

Tom: Nice? I thought it was awful! The weather wasn't very good, the people weren't friendly, and the hotel was terrible.

Alice: Oh? Well, Ben thought the restaurants were good.

Tom: Well, yeah, the restaurants were good. But they were really expensive and the service was slow!

PRONUNCIATION

🎙 1. Listen. Notice the difference in the pronunciation of *was* and *wasn't* and *were* and *weren't*.

The hotel was nice.
The restaurants were expensive.

The hotel wasn't nice.
The restaurants weren't expensive.

🎙 2. Now listen and check (✓) the sentences you hear.

☐ The people were friendly.
☐ The food was expensive.
☐ The streets were noisy.
☐ The weather was great.

☐ The people weren't friendly.
☐ The food wasn't expensive.
☐ The streets weren't noisy.
☐ The weather wasn't great.

3. *Pairs.* Student A, say a sentence in Exercise 2. Student B, point to the sentence you heard.

CONVERSATION

1. Practice the conversation.

    Alice: Was the nightlife good in New Orleans?

    Ben: Yeah, it was great. We went to lots of **jazz clubs**....

    Alice: Oh, were they any good?

    Ben: Well, the **music was fabulous**, but the **clubs were** really **crowded**.

    Alice: Yeah, I bet.

2. *Pairs.* Practice the conversation again. Use the cues.

DANCE CLUBS

music—good
dance floor—crowded

PARTIES

people—friendly
food—horrible

Business trips

How U.S. business people spend their free time on business trips:

1. using the hotel exercise facilities
2. working in their hotel rooms
3. shopping

LISTENING

📼 1. Listen to the rest of the conversation. Under each picture, write the day that Ben went to that place.

_____

_____

_____

_____

2. *Pairs.* Check your answers.

   Ⓐ He went to the casino on Thursday.
   Ⓑ Right. And he…

MAKE IT PERSONAL

1. *Pairs.* Interview your partner about a real or imaginary trip. Ask questions and take notes.

   Ⓐ How was your trip?
   Ⓑ My trip to (San Diego)? It was (great).
   Ⓐ Was the weather OK?

Name _____   Place _____   Weather _____

People _____   Hotel _____   Food _____

2. Tell the class about your partner's trip. For example, *Mario went to San Diego, California. The hotel was awful, but the weather was beautiful. Every day was sunny and warm.*

READING AND WRITING

1. Scan the restaurant review and answer these questions:
   a. Where is the restaurant?
   b. What kind of food do they serve?
   c. Is it expensive?

2. Read the review. *Pairs*. Discuss. Does the reviewer like the restaurant?

Where To Eat | Eliza Fitzgerald

The Courtyard is an inexpensive but beautiful little restaurant right in the middle of New Orleans' French Quarter. Don't miss it—it's excellent!

There is an outside courtyard with lots of plants and flowers and a beautiful little fountain in one corner. You can eat in the courtyard or in the small dining room, which is also full of plants. Some nights a jazz band plays in the courtyard.

The Courtyard is famous for its Creole food. On a recent visit, my friends and I tried all the specialties. Our favorites were the seafood jambalaya (rice with lobster, mussels, clams, and shrimp), blackened redfish (redfish grilled with lots of spices), and fresh red crayfish. The dirty rice (red beans and rice with or without sausage) was especially good. For dessert we had the specialty of the house—bread pudding in whiskey sauce. It was absolutely delicious!

The service was friendly and fast. Our server knew about all the food and its ingredients (one of my guests was a vegetarian). Our food arrived quickly and was served piping hot.

There were only two problems with the restaurant. We had to wait one hour for a table, and the courtyard was very, very noisy. If you want a quiet meal, eat inside.

The Courtyard ★ ★ ★

612 St. Louis Street
New Orleans, Louisiana
(504) 555-2815

Lunch: 11:30 a.m. to 3:00 p.m. Monday through Saturday
Dinner: 5:30 p.m. to 10:00 p.m. Sunday through Thursday;
6:00 p.m. to 11:00 p.m. Friday and Saturday
Appetizers: $4.25 – $6.95
Main Courses: $12.95 – $19.95
Credit Cards: Visa, MasterCard
Reservations not accepted
Wheelchair Access: No steps

★ Good
★ ★ Very Good
★ ★ ★ Excellent
★ ★ ★ ★ Extraordinary

3. Look at the pictures. Which one is The Courtyard?

a.

b.

c.

4. Look at the pictures. Which dishes are on The Courtyard's menu?

5. *Pairs.* Discuss. Imagine that you're in New Orleans. Would you like to go to The Courtyard for dinner? Why or why not? For example, *I'd like/ wouldn't like to go there because...*

6. There are five paragraphs in the restaurant review. Each paragraph has a topic. Match the topic to the paragraph.

___ food   __1__ overview   ___ problems   ___ decor   ___ service

7. *Pairs.* Tell your partner about your favorite restaurant. Be sure to talk about the decor, the food, and the service.

8. On a separate piece of paper, write a review of your favorite restaurant.

9. *Pairs.* Share your reviews.

LISTENING

1. *Pairs.* Look at the pictures and fill in the blanks with the correct number.
   Use: **1.** *Edmund Hillary and Tenzing Norgay;* **2.** *Athens, Greece;* **3.** *Uruguay;*
   4. *Orville and Wilbur Wright;* **5.** *1967;* **6.** *London, England;* **7.** *15¢;* **8.** *Ceylon
   (Sri Lanka), India, and Israel;* **9.** *Alexander Graham Bell.*

The first city to have a subway was __6__.

Hamburgers at the first McDonald's were ____.

The inventor of the telephone was ____.

The first men to fly were ____.

The first heart transplant was in ____.

The first modern Olympic Games were in ____.

The winner of the first World Cup was ____.

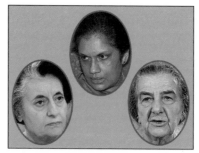

The first three women prime ministers were from ____.

The first men to climb Mt. Everest were ____.

2. Listen to the conversation and check your answers.

GRAMMAR		
When	**was**	the first heart transplant?
Who	**was**	the inventor of the telephone?
How much	**were**	hamburgers at the first McDonald's?
Where	**were**	the first three women prime ministers from?

CONVERSATION

🔲 Practice the conversation.

Pam: OK. And who was the first person to sail around the world?

Don: Oh, I know that one. It was Magellan, right?

Pam: Right. Ferdinand Magellan.

Don: When was that?

Pam: 1519.

Don: 1519, huh? Where was he from?

Pam: Portugal.

Don: Portugal? I didn't know that.

PRONUNCIATON

🔲 1. Listen. Notice the pronunciation of the initial consonant clusters with /r/. Then listen and repeat.

<u>br</u>own   <u>cr</u>owded   <u>dr</u>ink   <u>fr</u>om   <u>Gr</u>eece   <u>pr</u>ime   <u>tr</u>ansplant   <u>thr</u>ee

2. Now say these words.

bread   cross   draw   French   great   pretty   trip   throat

3. *Pairs.* Brainstorm as many words as you can that have initial consonant clusters with /r/.

TRY TO REMEMBER

1. *Pairs.* Look at the "firsts" on page 38. Write six questions. Use *who, what, when, where,* or *how much* with *was* and *were.* (Make sure you know the answers.)

2. *Two pairs.* Close your books. Take turns asking your questions. Score one point for each correct answer.

VOCABULARY

1. Listen to the conversations. Number the pictures to match.

romantic

funny

sad

violent

stupid

exciting

boring

scary

2. *Pairs.* Check your answers.

   Ⓐ Number 1 was boring.
   Ⓑ Right. And number 2 was….

3. *Pairs.* Brainstorm a list of movies now playing. Talk about the movies you know.

   Ⓐ I thought "Fireball" was really exciting.
   Ⓑ Me, too.
      OR
   Ⓑ Not me. I thought it was stupid.
      OR
   Ⓑ I didn't see it.

GRAMMAR

It was really	interesting,	**and**	the acting was excellent.
	violent,	**but**	

CONVERSATION

1. Practice the conversation.

Tina: What movie was that?
Rick: **Terminator 2.**
Tina: Oh, yeah? How was it?
Rick: It was great. It was really **exciting, and** the acting was excellent.
Tina: Really? Who was in it?
Rick: **Arnold Schwarzenegger and Linda Hamilton.**

2. *Pairs.* Practice the conversation again. Use these cues.

Jaws

Roy Scheider, Richard Dreyfuss

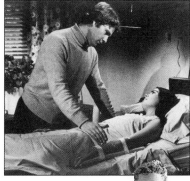

Love Story

Ryan O'Neal, Ali MacGraw

My Little Chickadee

Mae West, W.C. Fields

3. *Pairs.* Now have a conversation about a terrible movie.
   Student A, begin. For example, *"Robots from Mars" was on TV last night.*
   Student B, continue. For example, *Oh, yeah? How was it?*

MAKE IT PERSONAL

1. *Pairs.* Student A, tell your partner about the last movie you saw. Student B, begin: *What was the last movie you saw?* Take notes.

2. Report to the class. For example, *David saw "Frankenstein." He thought it was great, but it was really violent.*

READING AND WRITING

1. Look at the pictures. Cover the article. How old do you think these women are? Why do you think they are famous?

2. Read the article. Were your answers correct?

The Delany Sisters

The Broadway show *Having Our Say* was about two African-American sisters, Sarah "Sadie" Louise and Annie "Bessie" Elizabeth Delany. The show was based on their book, *Having Our Say: The Delany Sisters' First 100 Years*. When the book was published, Sadie was 101 years old and Bessie was 103.

Bessie and Sadie were born in North Carolina in the late 1800s. Their father, a former slave, became a college professor and was the first black Episcopal bishop in the United States.

Bessie and Sadie went to college in North Carolina and became teachers. In the 1920s, they moved to Harlem, a neighborhood in New York City. Bessie studied to become a dentist and was the only black person in her class. She later became a dental surgeon and was the first black female dentist in Harlem. Sadie was one of the first blacks to teach in the New York City public schools.

When they lived in Harlem, the sisters became friends with many famous black politicians, artists, and entertainers but they never married. "When people ask me how we've lived past 100," Bessie said, "I say, 'Honey, we never married. We never had husbands to worry us to death.'"

3. Label the pictures. Use these words: *Harlem, a college in North Carolina, Bessie and Sadie's friend, Bessie and Sadie's family.*

a. _____

b. _____

c. _____

d. _____

4. Brainstorm about a famous person (an actor, a musician, a historical figure, a politician, etc.), a family member, or classmate. Write as many facts as you can about the person.

5. On a separate piece of paper, write a biography about the person. Write at least three paragraphs.

6. *Pairs.* Share your biographies.

WORLD VIEW

Proverbs and sayings about old age

The tongue of experience has the most truth. —Arab

You can't teach an old dog new tricks. —English

Don't laugh at age…pray to reach it. —Chinese

Which proverb do you agree with most? Why?
What are some proverbs about old age in your language?

VOCABULARY

📼 1. What's the best place in the world to do these activities? Listen to the news report. Write the letter of the place next to the activity.

a. Hong Kong
b. San Diego, California, U.S.
c. Honolulu, Hawaii, U.S.
d. Rio de Janeiro, Brazil

e. Cancun, Mexico
f. Kathmandu, Nepal
g. Tahiti, Polynesia
h. Cairns, Australia

i. The French Alps
j. Quebec, Canada
k. Rome, Italy
l. Bermuda

1. go skiing __i__

2. go hiking ___

3. go biking ___

4. go swimming ___

5. go snorkeling ___

6. go surfing ___

7. go scuba diving ___

8. go sailing ___

9. go whale-watching ___

10. go shopping ___

11. go sightseeing ___

12. go dancing ___

2. *Pairs.* Check your answers.

Ⓐ What's the best place to go skiing?
Ⓑ The French Alps. What's the best place to…?

Personalize

3. *Pairs.* What's the best place to do these activities in your country? Take notes.

Ⓐ I think the best place to go dancing is….

We	**went**	surfing.	PRESENT	PAST
	didn't go	to Hawaii.	go	went
		to the beach.		

CONVERSATION

Practice the conversation.

Joe: Hi, Sharon. How was your vacation?

Sharon: It was great! We went to Honolulu.

Joe: Honolulu? Really?

Sharon: Yeah. We went to the beach. We went swimming, snorkeling…

Joe: What about surfing?

Sharon: No, we didn't go surfing, but we went scuba diving.

Joe: Wow! Sounds great.

FIND SOMEONE

1. Find someone who went to the same place as you on your vacation.

   (A) On my vacation, I went to Cancun. What about you?

   (B) I went to Cancun, too.

2. Find someone who did the same thing as you on your vacation.

   (A) On my vacation, I went snorkeling. What about you?

   (B) I didn't go snorkeling. I…

3. Report to the class. For example, *James and I both went to Cancun. Sheila and I both went snorkeling.*

In the United States, the top vacation places are:

1. Florida
2. California
3. Hawaii

Where do people in your country go on vacation?

GRAMMAR			Regular Verbs		Irregular Verbs	
I			**PRESENT**	**PAST**	**PRESENT**	**PAST**
You			stay	stayed	sleep	slept
He	**stayed**	home.	watch	watched	have	had
She			listen	listened	go	went
We	**read**	the newspaper.			eat	ate
They					read	read

CONVERSATION

🔲 Practice the conversation.

Wendy: Hi, Sam. How was your weekend?

Sam: It was OK, I guess. I didn't do much. I just stayed home, watched TV, listened to music, and read the newspaper. What about you?

Wendy: Well, my weekend was really hectic.

Sam: Oh, yeah? How come?

LISTENING

🔲 1. Listen to the rest of the conversation. Check (✓) the things Wendy did.

___ had a party

___ watched TV

___ cleaned the house

___ went shopping

___ listened to music

___ cooked

___ went jogging

___ slept late

___ played tennis

___ visited friends

___ studied for a test

___ ate out

2. *Pairs.* Check your answers.

Ⓐ She had a party.

Ⓑ Right. But she didn't watch TV.

PRONUNCIATION

1. Listen. Notice the pronunciation of *-ed*.

/t/	/d/	/ɪd/
looked	listened	visited
watched	played	

2. Put these verbs in the correct columns.

cleaned	cooked	helped	liked	lived
repeated	stayed	studied	talked	practiced

3. Listen and check your answers. Then say the verbs.

4. Make as many true sentences as you can about what you did last week. For example, *Last week, I watched TV. I...*

She was as busy as a bee.

INFORMATION EXCHANGE

What did she do last Monday?

Pairs.
Student A, go to page 118.
Student B, go to page 122.

MAKE IT PERSONAL

1. *Pairs.* Talk about a busy weekend. Say what you did Saturday and Sunday in the morning, afternoon, and evening. Use at least five different verbs. Begin, *Hi, _____. How was your weekend?*

2. Report to the class. For example, *Rona slept late on Saturday morning. She went to....*

READING AND WRITING

1. *Pairs.* Look at the map of Mexico and find Cancun. Brainstorm. What kinds of activities do you think you can do there?

<u>swimming</u>

_____

_____

_____

_____

_____

_____

_____

2. Look at the photos and read the letter on the next page. How many of the activities in Exercise 1 did Beth and Jack do? What other activities did they do?

Dear Shirley,   December 3

    You won't believe what Jack and I did last weekend! We went to Cancun!

    We got there early Friday morning, checked in, and went straight to the beach. We went scuba diving all morning, and we relaxed on the beach and swam all afternoon. Before dinner, we went shopping and then we had a wonderful Mexican meal. That night we went dancing in the hotel nightclub until 1a.m.

    On Saturday we went to Tulum, the Mayan ruins about two hours south of Cancun. On the way there, we stopped at a beautiful blue lagoon called Xelha, where we went snorkeling. The fish were fabulous! We had lunch on the beach, and in the afternoon we visited the ruins.

    On Sunday, we got up early again and had a fabulous Mexican breakfast near the pool. Then we rented a sailboat and went sailing. When we got back, people were parasailing on the beach. It looked dangerous, but I had to try it. It was a lot of fun!

    As soon as I came down from parasailing, we had to run to the hotel, check out, and get to the airport. We slept all the way home, but what a wonderful three days!

        Love, Beth

P.S. Here are a few photos. I'll send more later.

3. Read the letter again. How did Beth organize her ideas?

   a. by place   **b.** by time   **c.** by activity

4. Think about a vacation you went on recently, or use your imagination. On a separate piece of paper, write the days of the week and times of the day. Write notes about your activities. For example,

	morning	afternoon	evening
Thursday	went to Belize	rested	had dinner
Friday	went sightseeing	went shopping	went dancing
Saturday	played tennis	went hiking	went to sleep

5. On a separate piece of paper, write a letter to a friend about your vacation. Organize it by time.

6. *Pairs.* Share your letters.

Did she fly around the world?

LISTENING

The Life of Amelia Earhart

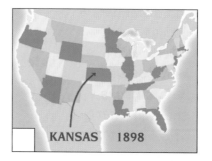
KANSAS 1898

a

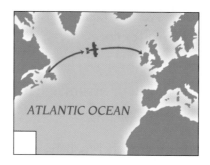
ATLANTIC OCEAN

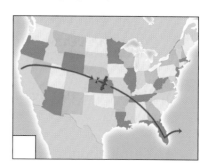

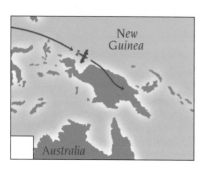
New Guinea

Australia

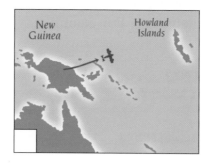
New Guinea

Howland Islands

1. *Pairs.* Match the sentences and the pictures.

    a. She learned to fly when she was 23 years old.
    b. She sent her last message at 8:45 A.M. on July 3. No one ever saw her again.
    c. At 10:30 A.M. on July 2, she took off for the Howland Islands in the middle of the Pacific Ocean.
    d. In 1922, she bought her first airplane.
    e. On May 21, 1937, she left California to fly around the world.
    f. Amelia Earhart was born in Kansas in 1898.
    g. On June 30, she arrived in New Guinea.
    h. In 1928, she became the first woman to fly across the Atlantic Ocean.

2. Listen to the biography and check your answers.

GRAMMAR

Did			Yes,	I	did.
	you see that show about Amelia Earhart?		No,	I	didn't.
	the plane crash?		Yes,	it	did.
			No,	it	didn't.

CONVERSATION

Practice the conversation.

Beth: Did you see that show about Amelia Earhart last night?

Greg: No. She was a famous pilot, wasn't she?

Beth: Uh-huh. She flew across the Atlantic.

Greg: Didn't she fly around the world, too?

Beth: Not exactly. She started her trip, but then she disappeared.

Greg: Really? Did the plane crash?

Beth: Well, they never found the plane, so no one really knows.

TRY TO REMEMBER

1. Fill in the blanks with the past tense forms.

   learn _____   take off _____   find _____

   buy _____   send _____   disappear _____

   become _____   fly _____   arrive _____

   leave _____   start _____   see _____

2. *Pairs.* Look at the information about Amelia Earhart. Write five questions with *Did she.* (Make sure you know the answers.) For example, *Did she fly across the Pacific Ocean?*

3. *Two pairs.* Cover page 50. Take turns asking your questions. Score one point for each correct answer.

CONVERSATION

1. Practice the conversation.

Cindy: You look tired. What did you
do last night?

Tim: I was out late. We went **to a
karaoke bar.**

Cindy: Oh, yeah? Who did you go with?

Tim: Just some friends.

Cindy: Where did you go?

Tim: To that place on Grant Street.
You know … what's-its-name.

Cindy: Oh, yeah, that place. Did
you have fun?

Tim: We sure did. **I sang** *Yesterday.*

2. *Pairs.* Practice the conversation again. Use the cues.

BOWLING

I bowled a 200 game.

DANCING

I learned a new line dance.

TO A COMEDY CLUB

We saw Jerry Creinfeld.

TO A JAZZ CLUB

We heard Max Washington.

PRONUNCIATION

1. Listen. Notice the pronunciation of *did you.*

What did you do last night?   How did you get there?
Who did you go with?   Did you get home late?

2. Now listen and fill in the blanks.

_____ see?

_____ have a good time?

_____ get there?

_____ go?

_____ eat?

3. Now say all the questions.

MAKE IT PERSONAL

1. *Pairs.* Take turns talking about something you did. Ask each other questions. Take notes.

Ⓐ What did you do last night?
Ⓑ Well, I didn't do anything last night. But last Thursday I went to the Yankees game.
Ⓐ Oh, really? Who did they play?
Ⓑ The Red Sox. The Yankees won.
Ⓐ Great! Who did you go with?

2. Report to the class. For example, *Karen went to a Yankees game with her sister and their cousins. The Yankees played the Red Sox and....*

READING AND WRITING

1. Sometimes stories entertain. Sometimes they teach a lesson. Read these three stories. Which do you think teaches a lesson? Which is funny? Which is a mystery?

The Disappearance of Judge Joseph Crater

Joseph Crater was a well-known judge in New York State. One day in 1930, he got a phone call at home and he became upset. That night he went to his office and got some papers. The next day, he went to the bank and got $5,100 in cash. Later that day, he went out to dinner with friends at Billy Haa's Chophouse. After dinner, he said good night and got into a taxi. No one ever saw him again.

The Hikers

One day two men were hiking in the woods. Suddenly they saw a huge black bear. One man immediately sat down, took off his backpack, and took out his sneakers. He began to take off his hiking boots. The other man looked at him and said, "Are you crazy? Do you think you can run faster than that bear?"
"No," replied the first man. "But I can run faster than you!"

The Sidewalk Cafe

Last week, on a warm summer day, I was walking by a restaurant in the middle of New York City and I saw a woman and a young boy sitting at a table outside on the sidewalk. As I walked by, I heard the woman say to the boy, "Come on, Johnny. Hurry up and eat your soup before it gets dirty."

2. *Pairs.* Compare your answers to the questions in Exercise 1. Say why. For example, *I think the first story … because….*

3. *Pairs.* Discuss. Which story did you like best? Why? For example, *I like the story about … because….*

4. On a separate piece of paper, write a story like the ones you just read or about something that happened to you.

5. *Pairs.* Share your stories.

WORLD VIEW

What people in the U.S. read

Here's what men and women read each day:

Men
1. newspaper
2. news magazine
3. book or magazine relating to work

Women
1. newspaper
2. women's magazine
3. novel

What did you read yesterday?

LISTENING

Strategy: Listening for the general idea

▭ 1. Listen to the song. Circle the adjective that describes the song.

funny   romantic   sad   happy   scary   violent

Strategy: Making inferences

▭ 2. Listen to the song again and answer the questions.

1. Who is "you" in the song?
   - **a.** his mother
   - **b.** his sweetheart (girlfriend)
   - **c.** his best friend

2. What happened?
   - **a.** the man and woman got married
   - **b.** the weather was sunny
   - **c.** the woman left the man

Strategy: Recognizing what you know

▭ 3. Listen to the song again. Fill in the blanks with all the words you know.

The other _____, dear, as _____ lay sleeping

I dreamed _____ held _____ in my arms

_____ _____ awoke, dear, I _____ mistaken

and _____ hung my _____ and cried.

You are _____ sunshine, _____ _____ sunshine,

You make _____ happy when skies _____ gray

You'll _____ know, dear, how much _____ love _____

_____ don't take _____ sunshine away.

You told me _____, dear, you really _____ me

And no one else could come _____.

_____ now you've left _____, and _____ another

You have shattered _____ my _____.

VOCABULARY LEARNING

Strategy: Learning antonyms (words that are opposite in meaning)

Look at these examples of antonyms:

great ←→ awful   slim ←→ heavy   woman ←→ man

Write antonyms for these words. (Hint: Look through Units 5–8.) Then check your answers with a partner.

quiet	friendly	early	long	intelligent
boring	first	expensive	funny	black

Strategy: Learning spelling rules

1. Look at the rules for spelling the verb + *-ing*. Then make a chart on a separate piece of paper. Add *-ing* to these verbs and put them in the correct column: *watch, ski, hike, snorkel, sail, dive, shop, dance,* and *jog.*

For most verbs, add *-ing*.	For verbs ending in *e*, drop the final *e*, and add *-ing*.	For verbs of one syllable ending in a single vowel + consonant, double the final consonant, and add *-ing*.
surfing	biking	swimming

2. *Pairs.* Check your answers.

3. Look at the rules for spelling the regular past tense. Then make a chart on a separate piece of paper. Make these verbs past tense and put them in the correct column: *bike, marry, play, clean, watch, visit, carry, dance, hike, live, practice, help, stay, cook,* and *repeat.*

For most verbs, add *-ed*.	For verbs ending in *e*, add *-d*.	For verbs ending in consonant + *y*, change the *y* to *i*, and add *-ed*.
listened	liked	studied

4. *Pairs.* Check your answers.

CONVERSATION MANAGEMENT

Strategy: Encouraging the speaker—Express interest and ask a question

Ⓐ I went to a great movie last night.
Ⓑ Oh, yeah? What did you see?

Express interest.   Ask a question.

1. Read the conversation. Fill in the blanks with the questions in the box.

What kind of music do they have there?	*How come?*
Where did you go?	*How was it?*

   A: I saw *Last Love* last night.

   B: Oh, yeah? _____

   A: I thought it was great, but it was very sad.

   B: Really? _____

   A: Well, the man left the woman and they never saw each other again.

   B: Oh, too bad.

   A: What did *you* do last night?

   B: I went dancing.

   A: Oh? _____

   B: To Badlands.

   A: Badlands? _____

   B: Country-western. It was a lot of fun.

2. Listen to the conversation and check your answers.

3. Practice the conversation.

Personalize

4. *Pairs.* Student A, tell Student B about something you did for fun (last night, last weekend, last week). Student B, encourage the speaker. Express interest and ask a question (*Oh, yeah?, Really?, Oh?, _____?*).

GRAMMAR LEARNING

Strategy: Reviewing

Find someone who…

1. You have 15 minutes. Ask Yes/No questions. When someone says *yes*, write the person's name and ask the information question. Write the answer. For example,

Ⓐ Did you get married last year?
Ⓑ Yes, I did.
Ⓐ When did you get married?
Ⓑ On June 24.

FIND SOMEONE WHO			
1. got married last year.	David	(when?)	June 24
2. watched TV last night.		(what?)	
3. went dancing last weekend.		(who?)	
4. ate out last weekend.		(where?)	
5. slept late on Saturday.		(how many hours?)	
6. visited another country last year.		(what?)	
7. was born in another city.		(where?)	
8. did something fun after school/work yesterday.		(what?)	
9. listened to music last night.		(what kind?)	
10. cooked dinner last night.		(what?)	
11. took a vacation last year.		(where?)	
12. was sick last week.		(how long?)	
13. had breakfast this morning.		(what?)	
14. was a student here last year.		(who/teacher?)	
15. saw a good movie last weekend.		(what?)	
16. read the newspaper this morning.		(which?)	
17. talked to someone in English last week.		(who?)	
18. was late to class today.		(how late?)	
19. went jogging last week.		(how many times?)	
20. was born in January.		(when?)	

2. Report to the class. For example, *David got married on June 24 last year.*

Strategy: Classifying   Go to page 121.

Where did you put the toothpaste?

VOCABULARY

1. Listen to the telephone conversation. Put a check (✓) next to the items you find in rooms at the Yokada Hotel.

✓ soap   __ towels and washcloths   __ shampoo   __ conditioner   __ hand lotion

__ mouthwash   __ a shower cap   __ a shoe cloth   __ a toothbrush   __ toothpaste

__ a razor   __ shaving cream   __ a robe   __ slippers   __ a hair dryer

__ an iron   __ a coffeemaker   __ bottled water   __ a mini-bar   __ a sewing kit

2. *Pairs.* Check your answers.

   Ⓐ There's soap.
   Ⓑ Right. And there are…

GRAMMAR

Could I have	an	iron?	We'll send	one	right up.	I'm sorry. We don't have	one.
	some	toothpaste?		some			any.
		towels?					

CONVERSATION

1. Practice the conversation.

> **Desk Clerk:** Front desk. May I help you?
> **Guest:** Hello. This is Room 211. Could I please have **an iron**?
> **Desk Clerk:** Of course. We'll send **one** right up.
> **Guest:** Oh, good. Thanks. And could I have **some extra towels**, too?
> **Desk Clerk:** Sure. We'll send **some** up with the iron.
> **Guest:** Great. Oh! And could I have **some bottled water**?
> **Desk Clerk:** I'm sorry, **ma'am**. We don't have **any**. But you can get **some** at the shops in the lobby.
> **Guest:** OK. Thank you.

2. *Pairs.* Role-play the conversation. Student A, you're the guest. Use these cues. Student B, you're the desk clerk. Use the information on page 60.

MAKE IT PERSONAL

1. *Pairs.* What do you usually find in a hotel room in your country? Decide together and fill in the chart.

You always find	You sometimes find	You never find

2. *Pairs.* Role-play. Student A, you're a guest in a hotel in your country. Call the desk clerk (Student B) and ask for one thing you need. Begin, *Hello. This is Room _____. Could I please have a/an/some...?*

GRAMMAR

in the corner of

on

over

under

in

CONVERSATION

Practice the conversation.

Ken: I can't find the shampoo. Where did you put it?

Betty: Um … I think I put it in the corner of the bathtub. Or maybe it's on the shelf over the toilet.

Ken: Well, it's not there.

Betty: Oh. Well, did you look under the sink?

Ken: Yeah. It's not there, either. And it's not on the counter.

Betty: Oh, wait a minute. Here it is. It's in the drawer with my underwear.

Ken: What's it doing in the drawer with your underwear?

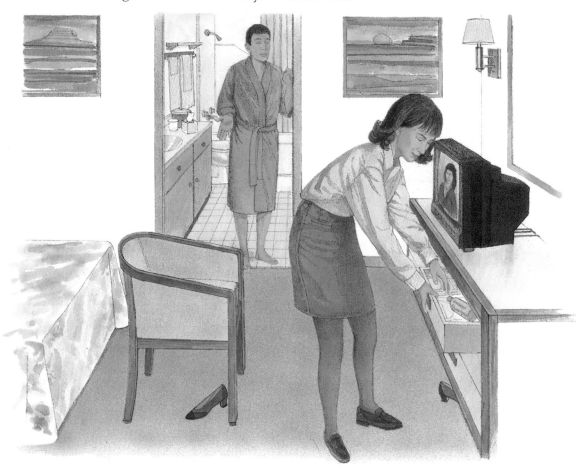

PRONUNCIATION

1. Listen. Notice the pronunciation of the compound nouns. Then say the words.

   ● ·   ● ● ·   ● ·

washcloth   hand lotion   mouthwash

2. Listen and mark the stressed syllables. Then say the words.

   shower cap   toothbrush   coffeemaker

3. Now say these words.

   hair dryer   toothpaste   bathtub   shoe cloth

LISTENING

1. Listen to the rest of the conversation. Write these things in the correct place in the hotel room on page 62:

   toothpaste   hair dryer   shower cap   mouthwash

2. *Pairs.* Check your answers.

   Ⓐ Where did you put the toothpaste?
   Ⓑ In the…

WORLD VIEW

Most important hotel items for U.S. business travelers:

1. alarm clock   3. coffeemaker
2. morning newspaper   4. minibar

What is most important to you?

INFORMATION EXCHANGE

It's right under your nose.

Where's the soap?

Pairs.
Student A, go to page 127.
Student B, go to page 124.

READING AND WRITING

1. Skim the message. What do you think Jim does?

   a. He's a tennis player.   **b.** He's a hotel clerk.   **c.** He's a travel agent.

> Jim,
>
>   Meg Shaw called. She and her family want to go to Bar Harbor, Maine, from July 19 to 26. Their children are three and five, so they need baby-sitting. They want a hotel with a restaurant, but they'd also really like a refrigerator in the room. Laundry facilities are a must.
>   The Shaws are big on exercise. They like to play tennis and swim, and they really want a health club.
>   They'd like to spend under $1,000 for the week. Please call Meg with some recommendations. Her number is 721-8297.
>   Nellie

2. Look at the symbols and match them to their meanings.

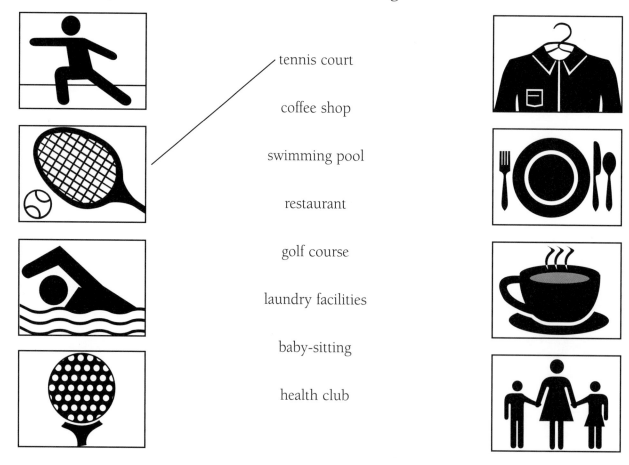

tennis court

coffee shop

swimming pool

restaurant

golf course

laundry facilities

baby-sitting

health club

3. *Pairs.* Look at the hotel ads. Discuss. Which hotel do you think is best for the Shaw family? Why? For example, *I think … is the best hotel for the Shaw family because…*

Harbor Inn

Comfortable and convenient. Located just a short 1/2 mile walk from the downtown/waterfront and one mile from Acadia National Park.

Special amenities include:
- king- or queen-size beds
- some kitchenette units
- remote control cable TV
- baby-sitting available

2 Person/1Bedroom $95–$115
Extra person $15

Will's Motel

Rural area, all drive-up units. Convenient and economical.

- free movies/cable TV
- coffee shop
- children under 12 stay for free
- some rooms have refrigerators
- restaurant nearby

2 Person/1Bedroom $46
Extra person $5

The Acadia Guest House

Overlooking Frenchman's Bay, near boating, downtown shopping, and Acadia National Park.

- some rooms have kitchens
- free movies/cable TV
- baby-sitting available

2 Person/1Bedroom $120–$175
Extra person $20

4. *Pairs.* Take turns. Student A, you're taking a trip and need a hotel. Call your travel agency and tell the receptionist (Student B) what you need, when, where, and how much you want to spend. Student B, take the message on a separate piece of paper.

5. *Pairs.* Read your message to your partner. Did you get the message right?

10   What's she doing?

GRAMMAR

What	's	he	doing?	He	's	robbing the apartment.
		she		She		
	are	they		They	're	

CONVERSATION

Practice the conversation.

John: What are you looking at?

Cathy: There's a strange woman in the Martinellis' apartment.

John: So? What's she doing?

Cathy: I think she's robbing the apartment.

John: You're kidding!

Cathy: No. She's taking a picture off the wall.

LISTENING

1. *Pairs.* Match the sentences and the pictures.

    a. She's opening the safe.
    b. She's putting the picture back on the wall.
    c. She's sitting down at the table and writing something.
    d. She's closing the safe.
    e. She's taking a box out of a bag.
    f. She's putting the picture on the table.
    g. She's leaving the note on the table.
    h. She's putting the box in the safe.

2. Listen to the rest of the conversation between John and Cathy and check your answers.

3. What do you think she's writing in her note? Guess. Then go to page 131 and read the note.

To make a long story short…

INFORMATION EXCHANGE

What's the story?

Pairs.
Student A, go to page 126.
Student B, go to page 129.

GRAMMAR

Am	I			you	are.		you	aren't.
Is	he	interrupting anything?		he	is.		he	isn't.
	she		Yes,	she		No,	she	
Are	they	reading the newspaper?		they	are.		they	aren't.
	you			I	am.		I	'm not.

CONVERSATION

Practice the conversation.

Darryl: Hello?

Tami: Hi, Darryl. This is Tami. Am I interrupting anything? Are you **watching the game?**

Darryl: Uh-uh. My roommate is. I'm just **reading the paper.**

Tami: Oh. Well, do you have **Yolanda's** phone number?

Darryl: Uh-huh. Just a minute.

PRONUNCIATION

In informal situations, you can use
"Uh-huh" for "Yes" and "Uh-uh" for "No."

1. Listen. Notice the difference in the pronunciation of *Uh-huh* and *Uh-uh*. Then listen and repeat.

2. Listen. If you hear *Yes*, say *Uh-huh*. If you hear *No*, say *Uh-uh*.

3. Listen. Check *Yes* for *Uh-huh* or *No* for *Uh-uh*.

		Yes	No
a.	Is Sal studying now?	☐	☑
b.	Is David talking on the phone?	☐	☐
c.	Are Kate and Tanya still sleeping?	☐	☐
d.	Is Pam watching TV?	☐	☐
e.	Are Jeff and Martin washing the car?	☐	☐
f.	Is Tim doing his homework?	☐	☐

4. *Pairs.* Check your answers.

Ⓐ Is Sal studying now?
Ⓑ Uh-uh.

LISTENING

 1. Listen to four more conversations between Darryl and Tami. Number the pictures to match the conversations.

2. *Pairs.* Practice the conversation again. Use the activities in Exercise 1. Use your own names and ask for another classmate's phone number.

WORLD VIEW

Where *No* means *Yes*

The body language for *yes* and *no* is different in different countries. For example, the up-and-down nod that means *yes* in the United States and most of Europe means *no* in parts of Greece, Turkey, Iran, and Bulgaria.

What is the body language for *yes* and *no* in your country?

WHAT AM I DOING?

Groups. Take turns performing an action and guessing what your classmate is doing.

READING AND WRITING

1. *Pairs.* Look at the headline and the picture. Cover the article. Predict. What do you think the article is about?

2. *Pairs.* Write three questions you want the article to answer.

3. Read the article. Was your prediction correct? Were your questions answered?

Royal Crown Stolen
Police are Questioning Suspects

The fabulous Royal Crown, on display at the Museum of Fine Art in Dallas, is now missing. The ruby and diamond crown, said to belong to Queen Isabella of Spain and valued at over $2,000,000, was found last year in the sunken pirate ship, "The Avenger."

According to museum director Pat Weber, the crown was in a special case in the center of a small room with only one door, which was locked. There were no windows. "Security was excellent," Mr. Weber said. "A guard was outside the door 24 hours a day. There was a video camera on the crown at all times."

The head of security for the museum said they were completely baffled. "When we got to the room this morning, nothing was unusual. The security guard was on duty, and the door was locked. When we unlocked the door, the crown was missing and there was a cloth over the video camera. It's just impossible! The video camera was 20 feet up on the wall."

Police are searching for clues. "We are interviewing all the people at the museum today," Police Chief Roger Bryce said. "We are working around the clock, and we won't rest until we find the crown."

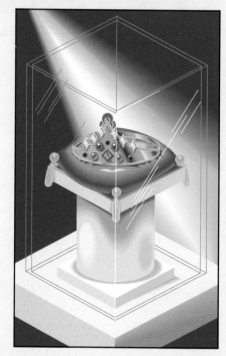

4. Which picture shows the room before the thief stole the crown?

 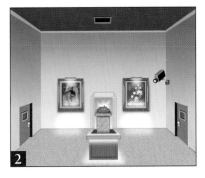 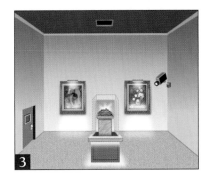

5. *Pairs.* Check your answer with a partner. Explain your choice. For example, *It isn't picture number … because….*

6. How did the thief steal the crown? Look at the pictures and write a paragraph. Begin: *First, the thief opened the air-conditioning vent. He climbed down a long rope into the room. Then…*

7. *Pairs.* Share your paragraphs.

What are you studying?

VOCABULARY

1. Listen to the news report and fill in the graph.

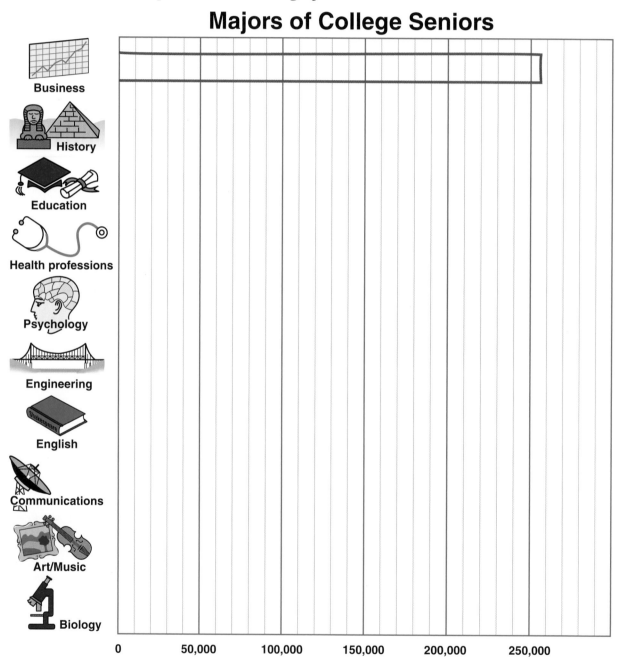

Majors of College Seniors

Business

History

Education

Health professions

Psychology

Engineering

English

Communications

Art/Music

Biology

0   50,000   100,000   150,000   200,000   250,000

2. *Pairs.* Check your answers.

Ⓐ 257,000 seniors are majoring in business.

Ⓑ Right. And…

GRAMMAR

I'm	studying	history.
	majoring in	

CONVERSATION

1. Practice the conversation.

Melissa: Hi. It's great to see you!

Eric: Same here. What are you doing now?

Melissa: I'm studying at the University of **Arizona**.

Eric: Oh, yeah? Do you like it?

Melissa: Yeah. It's hard work, but it's interesting.

Eric: What's your major?

Melissa: **Engineering** ... for now. What about you?

Eric: Oh, I'm studying at **the University of Colorado**. I'm majoring in **communications**.

2. *Pairs.* Role-play. You are one of the people at the game. Have a conversation like the one between Melissa and Eric.

TAKE A SURVEY

1. Ask three classmates, *What are/were your favorite subjects in school?*

Name:	Judy		
Favorite Subjects:	biology history		

2. Report to the class. For example, *Judy's favorite subjects were biology and history.*

GRAMMAR		
How		doing?
Where	are you	working?
What department		working in?

CONVERSATION

Practice the conversation.

Bill: Hi, Norma. How are you doing?

Norma: Fine. How about you?

Bill: Just great. I hear you're living in Springfield now.

Norma: Uh-huh. We just moved there. I just got a new job.

Bill: Oh, really? Where are you working?

Norma: I'm working for Berry Computer.

Bill: Berry? What department are you working in?

Norma: Software development. It's really a great job.

LISTENING

1. Listen to the rest of the conversation. Who is doing what? Label the pictures with the names *Don, Kate, Susie,* or *Bill* and answer the questions.

Start a new business	Apply to law school	Interview for a job	Travel

Who? _____	Who? __Don__	Who? _____	Who? _____
What kind?	Which school?	Where?	Who with?

2. *Pairs.* Check your answers.

    Ⓐ Who's applying to law school?

    Ⓑ Don.

    Ⓐ Which law schools is he applying to?

PRONUNCIATION

1. Listen. Notice the reduction of *are you* in these information questions.

What are you doing now?
Where are you studying?
How are you doing?
Who are you going with?

2. Listen and write the questions.

1. _____?
2. _____?
3. _____?
4. _____?

3. *Pairs.* Check your answers.

Ⓐ Number 1 is *How are you going?*
Ⓑ Right. And number 2 is…

4. Now say the questions in Exercises 1 and 2.

MAKE IT PERSONAL

1. *Pairs.* Have a conversation. Greet each other. Then ask, What are you doing now?

2. Report to the class. For example, Mike is living in Springfield. He's working for Ford. He's studying photography at night at Springfield Community College.

Me? I'm writing a symphony, finishing my ninth novel, learning to fly, working on a cure for cancer, and running marathons. How about you?

READING AND WRITING

1. *Pairs.* Cover the article. Write this sentence on a separate piece of paper and complete it with as many ideas as you can. *A good language learner is someone who…*

2. Read the article. Check (✓) the ideas that are the same as yours.

How To Be a Good Language Learner

Recently we talked to Dr. Rob Gilbert, author of *The List that Can Save Your Life: Secret Insights to College Success.* According to Dr. Gilbert, here are the ten most important things a student must do to be a good language learner.

1. Always go to class.
2. Get to class early.
3. Sit in the middle of the front row.
4. Sit up straight and pay attention.
5. Ask and answer questions.
6. Study every day. Don't cram.
7. Learn something new every day.
8. Do <u>all</u> homework assignments and submit them on time.
9. Use your new language outside of class at least once every day.
10. Don't quit, no matter what!

3. Look at the dictionary entries for *cram*, *submit*, and *quit* from the *Oxford ESL Dictionary for Students of American English*. Notice that each word has several meanings. Find the word in the article, and then circle the number of the appropriate meaning in the dictionary.

> mass of rock.
> **craggy** *adj* (-ier, -iest) having many crags
> **cram** /kræm/ *vt, vi* (-mm-) **1** ***cram into/with,*** make too full; put, push, very much or too much into: *to ~ food into one's mouth/~ one's mouth with food; to ~ papers into a drawer.* **2** study or learn hastily (for an examination).
> **cramp** /kræmp/ *n* **1** [C,U] sudden and painful tightening of the muscles, usu caused by cold

> quit /kwit/ *adj* free, clear: *We are well ~ of him.* fortunate to be rid of him.
> **quit** /kwit/ *vt, vi* (*pt, pp~*, ~ted, *pres p* -tt-) **1** stop or give up doing something; cease (from): *The athlete will never ~ until he wins. Quit pestering me!* **2** go away from; leave: *The enemy soldiers ~ the town. The club made too many demands on his time, so he ~.*
> **quit•ter** *n* [C] (*informal*) person who does not finish what he has started.

> **sub•miss•ive•ness** /-nɪs/ *n* [U]
> **sub•mit** /səb'mɪt/ *vt, vi* (-tt-) **1** put (oneself) under the control of another: *~ oneself to discipline.* **2** put forward for opinion, discussion, decision, etc: *~ plans/proposals to a committee.* **3** (*legal*) suggest: *Counsel ~ted that there was no case against his client.* **4** surrender: *~ to separation from one's family.*
> **sub•nor•mal** /səb'normal/ *adj* below normal

4. *Pairs.* Make a list like Dr. Gilbert's. Use your ideas from Exercise 1. Add other ideas from the article. Then compare your list with another pair's.

5. Which things on your list do you do now? Check them.

6. Write yourself a list of things you plan to do from now on. For example, TO DO: Get to class early.

7. *Pairs.* Share your "To Do" lists.

TO DO: _____

___ Get to class early. ___

_____

_____

_____

_____

_____

Unit 12

We're going to fly to Honolulu.

VOCABULARY

1. Listen to the radio advertisement and fill in the blanks. Use these words:
   camp, climb, drive, fly, go, play, relax, rent, sail, stay, take.

1. _fly_ to Honolulu

2. _____ at the Hilton

3. _____ on the beach

4. _____ to Maui

5. _____ a car

6. _____ around the island

7. _____ on the beach

8. _____ a helicopter tour

9. _____ a volcano

10. _____ whale-watching

11. _____ golf

12. _____ snorkeling

2. *Pairs.* Check your answers.

Ⓐ Number 1 is fly to Honolulu.
Ⓑ Right. And number 2 is…

GRAMMAR

I	'm		
We	're	**going to**	**fly** to Honolulu.
He	's		

CONVERSATION

1. Practice the conversation.

Marc: Guess what! Doris and I are going to go to Hawaii for our anniversary!

Yvette: You are? That's fantastic!

Marc: Yeah! First, we're going to fly to Honolulu and stay at the Hilton for three days.

Yvette: The Hilton? Wow!

Marc: Yeah. We're just going to relax on the beach for a few days.

Yvette: Then what?

Marc: Then we're going to sail to Maui, rent a car, and drive around the island.

2. *Pairs*. Role-play. Continue the conversation. Use the information on page 78 and prompts, such as *And then what are you going to do?* or *Then what?*

PRONUNCIATION

1. Listen. Notice that the pronunciation of *going to* before a verb is "gonna" in fast speech.

I'm going to drive there. (slow)   I'm going to (gonna) drive there. (fast)

2. Listen. After each sentence write *F* for *Fast* or *S* for *Slow*.

1. He's going to fly to Hawaii. ___

2. They're going to stay at the Hilton. ___

3. I'm going to rent a car. ___

4. She's going to sail to Maui. ___

5. We're going to play golf. ___

6. You're going to be late. ___

She's going nowhere fast.

INFORMATION EXCHANGE

Where is she going?

Pairs.
Student A, go to page 125.
Student B, go to page 128.

GRAMMAR		
When		come back?
Where		stay?
Who	**are you going to**	go with?
How		get there?
How long		be away?

CONVERSATION

1. Practice the conversation.

Abby: When are you going to take your vacation this year?

Marty: In the **spring**. I'm going to go to **Quebec City**.

Abby: Really? That sounds great. How are you going to get there?

Marty: By **bus**. It's a long trip, but I have plenty of time.

Abby: Oh. How long are you going to be away?

Marty: **Almost a month.**

Abby: Wow! Where are you going to stay?

Marty: At a **little inn right in the middle of the city.**

Abby: Sounds wonderful!

2. *Pairs.* Practice the conversation again. Use the cues.

This Fall, Visit Beautiful Santa Fe, New Mexico

TAKE THE TRAIN TOURS!

Special Fall Tour: October 11–31

Stay at the **Old Savoy Hotel** in the middle of downtown Santa Fe

Only $750 (per person, double occupancy)
Includes transportation

Call (800) 979-0834 for reservations

Fly California Airlines to LOS ANGELES

Special Winter Rates December 1–7

Stay at the **Funworld Hotel** right in the middle of Los Angeles

Only $510 (per person, double occupancy—Children free!)

Call (800) 294-5800

Mayflower Lines
Summer Cruise to Alaska

Leave Seattle: July 7
Return to Seattle: July 16
Accommodations:
7 nights on the cruise ship
3 nights at the Crown Hotel in downtown Anchorage

Only $2,500 (per person, double occupancy)

Call (800) 750-6602 for reservations

LISTENING

1. Listen to the rest of the conversation. Circle the correct answers.

When?	in the spring	in the summer	in the fall	in the winter
Where?	Buenos Aires	Rio de Janeiro	Russia	Japan
How long?	7 days	10 days	14 days	21 days
Who/with?	her mother	her parents	her sister	her friend
What?	relax on the beach	go scuba diving	go swimming	go shopping
	go dancing	go to museums	go to nightclubs	go sightseeing

2. *Pairs.* Check your answers.

   Ⓐ When is she going to take her vacation?

   Ⓑ In the fall. Where is she going to go?

MAKE IT PERSONAL

1. Plan your ideal vacation. Decide when you want to go, where, for how long, etc.

2. *Pairs.* Ask your partner about his or her ideal vacation. Use *when? where? who/with? what? how? how long?*, etc. Take notes.

3. Report to the class. For example, *Julie is going to visit Timbuktu on her next vacation. She's going to....*

WORLD VIEW

What would you take with you on an ideal vacation?

Here's what people in the United States said:

1. a romantic companion
2. a swimsuit
3. evening clothes

What would you take?

READING AND WRITING

1. You want to go sightseeing in Europe on your next vacation. You have three weeks and $2,000 to spend. You want to stay in good hotels, and you don't want to pay extra for your meals. Skim this brochure. Is this a good tour for you? On a separate piece of paper, list all the reasons. Compare your list with a partner's.

18-DAY

CAPITAL CITIES TOUR

London, Amsterdam, Paris,
Madrid, Rome, Vienna
from $1,800

FIRST CLASS HOTELS

Double rooms with private bath. All service charges, local taxes, baggage handling, and hotel tips included.

DINING AND ENTERTAINMENT

Welcome drink in London. Continental breakfast and dinner included throughout the tour.

TRANSPORTATION

All tours of the cities in luxury air-conditioned buses with rest rooms.

TOUR GUIDES

Professional multilingual tour director. Specialized local guides in each capital.

London Visit the Tower of London, Buckingham Palace, the British Museum, and Westminster Abbey. Enjoy an evening at the theater.

Amsterdam Take a boat ride on the canals. Visit Anne Frank's House, the Heineken Brewery, and the Van Gogh Museum.

Paris Visit the Eiffel Tower, the Louvre, and Notre Dame Cathedral. Shop on the famous Champs Elysees and the fashionable Rue de Rivoli. Spend an evening at the Moulin Rouge.

Madrid Go to a bullfight and explore the Prado Museum, the Royal Palace, and the Plaza Mayor. Dine in an authentic Spanish restaurant and watch flamenco dancers.

Rome Go to the Coliseum, St. Peter's Basilica, the Roman Forum, and the Spanish Steps. Shop on the famous Via Veneta and go out for an authentic Italian dinner.

Vienna Visit St. Stephen's Cathedral, the Hofberg, and Belvedere Palace Gardens. Tour the old city in a horse-drawn carriage and spend an evening listening to the music of Mozart.

2. Label the pictures with the cities on the tour.

a. _____   b. _____

c. _____   d. _____

e. _____   f. _____

3. Imagine that you're going on this tour. Write a letter to a friend and tell him or her what you're going to do.

4. *Pairs.* Share your letters.

VOCABULARY LEARNING

Strategy: Making flash cards

For example:

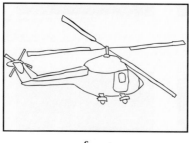

front   back

1. Make flash cards for these words.

Nouns	**Verbs**
a toothbrush	sail
an iron	fly
a whale	golf
a box	
a volcano	
a safe	
a razor	

2. *Pairs.* Student A, show a picture to Student B. Student B, say the word.

Strategy: Writing true sentences

1. Look through Units 9–12. Find ten words you want to remember.
   For each word, write a true sentence. Use a separate piece of paper.

   For example: engineering

   Ken is majoring in engineering.

2. *Pairs.* Read your sentences to each other.

LISTENING

Strategy: Getting meaning from context (the other words you hear)

1. Listen to the conversation. What does the word *twins* mean? Guess the meaning from the context.

2. Now listen to these conversations. Choose the picture that shows the meaning of each word.

1. kids   a.   b.   c.

2. ice   a.   b.   c.

3. vases   a.   b.   c.

Strategy: Getting the main idea

1. Listen to the news report. Circle the headline that matches.

Biggest Bank Robbery in History: $10,000,000 Missing

THIEVES ROB FAMOUS JEWELRY STORE: $10,000,000 in Cash and Jewelry Missing

Police Find Three Men Tied Up in Mercedes

Foreign Investors Purchase Goldsmith's for $10 Million

2. Listen again. Write three words that helped you choose the headline.

_____   _____   _____

CONVERSATION MANAGEMENT

Strategies: Keeping the conversation going—Answer and add

1. Read the two conversations. Notice that in Conversation 1, B "kills the conversation" each time he or she speaks. How? In Conversation 2, B keeps the conversation going each time. How?

CONVERSATION 1

A: Gee, it's nice to see you, Pat. So, tell me, what are you doing now?

B: I'm working.

A: Oh. Where?

B: In the travel department at American Express.

A: That's great! Do you like it?

B: Yeah.

A: Well ... that's good. Are you still taking classes?

B: Yes.

A: Uh ... that's nice. Good luck.

B: Thanks.

CONVERSATION 2

A: Gee, it's nice to see you, Pat. So, tell me, what are you doing now?

B: I'm working in the travel department at American Express.

A: That's great. Do you like it?

B: Oh, yeah. The work is really interesting, and I get to travel.

A: Well, that's terrific. Are you still taking classes?

B: Uh-huh. I'm going for my master's degree in business.

A: Hey, that's great! Good luck.

B: Thanks. Take care.

2. *Pairs.* Read the conversation. Add at least one sentence after each of B's answers. Then role-play the conversation.

A: Do you like to go dancing?

B: Yes. <u>I like it a lot.</u> _____

A: Where do you go?

B: To The Broadway. _____

A: Oh, yeah? Do you go very often?

B: Yes. _____

A: Do you go alone?

B: No. _____

3. *Pairs.* Talk about what you are going to do next weekend. Remember to keep the conversation going.

GRAMMAR LEARNING

Strategy: Reviewing

Groups of four. Use one book.

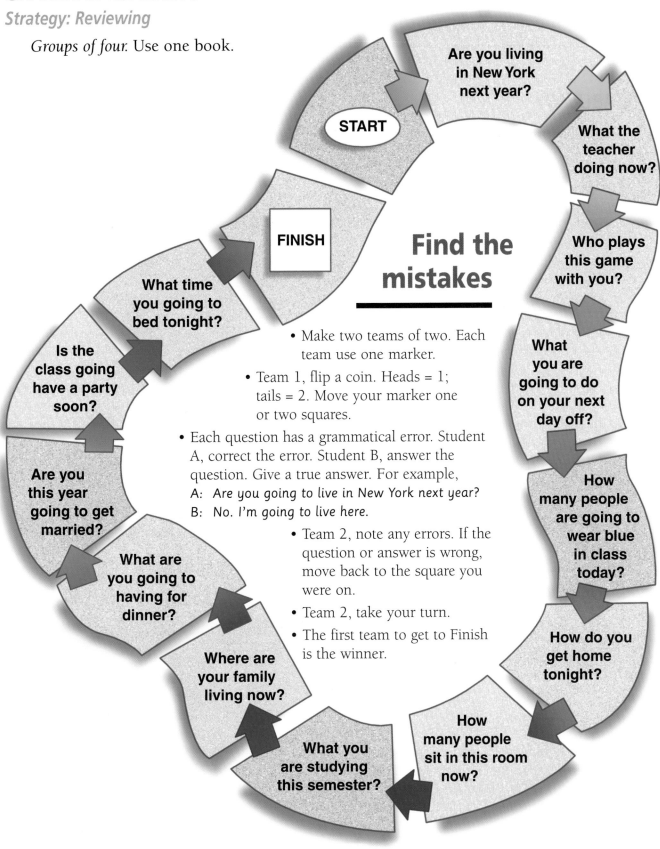

START

FINISH

Are you living in New York next year?

What the teacher doing now?

Who plays this game with you?

What you are going to do on your next day off?

How many people are going to wear blue in class today?

How do you get home tonight?

How many people sit in this room now?

What you are studying this semester?

Where are your family living now?

What are you going to having for dinner?

Are you this year going to get married?

Is the class going have a party soon?

What time you going to bed tonight?

Find the mistakes

- Make two teams of two. Each team use one marker.
- Team 1, flip a coin. Heads = 1; tails = 2. Move your marker one or two squares.
- Each question has a grammatical error. Student A, correct the error. Student B, answer the question. Give a true answer. For example,
  A: Are you going to live in New York next year?
  B: No. I'm going to live here.
- Team 2, note any errors. If the question or answer is wrong, move back to the square you were on.
- Team 2, take your turn.
- The first team to get to Finish is the winner.

Strategy: Keeping a grammar journal   Go to page 123.

13   I'm going on a picnic.

VOCABULARY

📼 1. Listen to the radio program. Number the foods in the correct order.

The Ten Most Popular Foods for Your Fourth of July Picnic

___ hamburgers

___ hot dogs

___ potato salad

___ watermelon

10 baked beans

___ barbecued chicken

___ corn on the cob

___ coleslaw

___ chocolate brownies

___ chips and dip

2. *Pairs.* Check your answers.

   Ⓐ The number 10 food is baked beans.
   Ⓑ Right. And the number 9 food….

	Are you doing anything special		
What	**are you doing**	on the 4th of July?	**I'm (not) going** on a picnic.

CONVERSATION

 1. Practice the conversation.

> Jill: Are you doing anything special for the Fourth of July?
>
> Rob: Uh-huh. I'm going on a picnic.
>
> Jill: Oh, yeah? Me, too. Who are you going with?
>
> Rob: Just some friends. We're going to Franklin Park.
>
> Jill: That sounds like fun. What are you having?
>
> Rob: Oh, the usual. **Hot dogs, baked beans, potato salad, coleslaw, and apple pie.**
>
> Jill: Mmmm!

2. *Pairs.* Practice the conversation again. Use other foods on page 88.

Favorite picnic foods

Mexico:	**Japan:**	**France:**
quesadilla	rice balls	cheese
avocado	grilled chicken	fruit

What are your favorite picnic foods?

MAKE IT PERSONAL

1. *Pairs.* Ask about your partner's weekend plans. Then ask for more information using *who, what, where,* and *when.*

   Ⓐ Are you doing anything special this weekend?
   Ⓑ Yeah. I'm going skiing.
   Ⓐ Oh, yeah? Who are you going with?

2. Report to the class. For example, *Stephanie is going skiing this weekend with...*

LISTENING

1. Listen to the conversations. Check (✓) the news for each person or couple.

What's the News?	Having a Baby	Moving to Denver	Getting a Promotion	Retiring	Graduating
Tony and Mary		✔			
Fran					
Betty					
Bill and Alice					
Mike					

2. Pairs. Check your answers.

 Ⓐ Who's having a baby?
 Ⓑ Bill and Alice. And who's…

GRAMMAR

	Jenny?		her?	
	Bob?		him?	
Did you hear about	the picnic?	No. What about	it?	
	Lynn and Ed?		them?	
	Mike and me?		you?	
		They didn't tell	me / us	about it.

CONVERSATION

Practice the conversation.

Mark: Hey, **Debbie**. How are you doing?
Debbie: Great! Did you hear the news about **Ed and Lynn?**
Mark: No. What about **them?**
Debbie: **They're getting married!**
Mark: No kidding! I just saw **them,** and **they** didn't tell me about it.
Debbie: Well, **they are,** and I'm having a party for **them** next week. Can you come?
Mark: Sure!

PRONUNCIATION

1. Listen. Notice the pronunciation of *him*, *her*, and *them*.

We're meeting (h)im tomorrow
We're meeting (h)er tomorrow.
We're meeting (th)em tomorrow.

2. Listen and fill in the blanks with *him, her*, or *them*.

1. We're having a party for ____him____ at the office.

2. I'm seeing _____ later.

3. We're visiting _____ tonight.

4. Nancy is taking _____ to the airport.

5. Mike is speaking to _____ tomorrow.

3. *Pairs.* Check your answers.

Ⓐ Number 1 is *him*.
Ⓑ Right. And number 2 is....

4. Now say the sentences in Exercise 2.

5. *Pairs.* Practice the conversation between Mark and Debbie again. Use the information in the chart on page 90.

MAKE IT PERSONAL

1. *Pairs.* Tell your partner some news about a famous person or someone you know. For example, *My friend Ann is backpacking in Europe this summer.*

2. Report to the class. For example, *Ken's friend Ann is backpacking in Europe this summer.*

READING AND WRITING

1. *Pairs.* What do people in your country do on New Year's Eve and New Year's Day? Write at least three things. Then read the article.

On New Year's Eve in Mexico, people wait for the clocks to strike midnight. At the first sound of the bells, people begin to eat grapes. They must eat 12 grapes before the bells ring 12 times.

In Japan, people eat special foods, including chewy rice cakes called *mochi*. Traditionally, men pound the rice to make mochi.

In the South of the United States, people eat black-eyed peas on New Year's Day. Some people think you have to eat 365 peas to have good luck every day of the new year.

New Year's Around The World

In most cultures, people celebrate the new year on January 1.

However, in some cultures, the new year begins on a different date. For example, the Chinese new year is in late January or early February, the Jewish new year is in September or October, and the Islamic new year is usually in May.

Different cultures have different ways of celebrating the new year. Most of these customs are observed to bring good luck.

In France, people eat oysters and drink white wine on New Year's Day.

In Greece, people throw old things such as plates, glasses, and even furniture out of the window on New Year's Day.

All over the United States, people have parties on New Year's Eve. At midnight, they drink champagne and kiss.

2. Vocabulary in context. Find the following words in the article. Re-read the paragraph, and guess the meaning of the words from context. Tell a classmate what you think the words mean.

celebrate   good luck   strike   kiss

3. Write about the customs for three holidays in your country. Don't write the name of the holiday (leave a blank). For example:

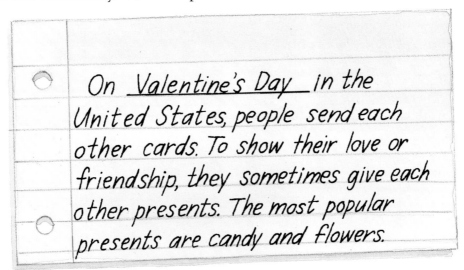

On_____in the United States, people send each other cards. To show their love or friendship, they sometimes give each other presents. The most popular presents are candy and flowers.

4. *Pairs.* Exchange papers. Read your partner's paper and fill in the blanks with the correct holiday. For example:

On _Valentine's Day_ in the United States, people send each other cards. To show their love or friendship, they sometimes give each other presents. The most popular presents are candy and flowers.

5. Check your answers with your partner.

VOCABULARY

🔊 1. Listen to the conversations and number the pictures to match. Brad is inviting his coworkers to a party.

I have to get up early tomorrow.

I have to study.

I have a headache.

I have to work late.

I have a doctor's appointment.

I have to go to class.

I have other plans.

I have to walk the dog.

I'm too tired.

2. *Pairs.* Check your answers.

Ⓐ What's the first excuse?

Ⓑ It's "I have to get up early tomorrow."

CONVERSATION

Practice the conversation.

Cliff: Hey, **Meg.** I'm going to a party. Do you want to come?

Meg: Oh, I'd love to, but I can't. **I have to work late.** Why don't you ask **Mike?**

Cliff: I did. **He** can't go, either. **He has to go to class.**

Meg: Oh, well. Maybe next time.

PRONUNCIATION

1. Listen. Notice the pronunciation of *have a*, *have to*, *has a*, and *has to*.

   I have a headache.   I have to study.
   He has a class tonight.   He has to work late.

2. Listen. Write the excuses. Use a separate piece of paper. Then say the excuses.

3. *Pairs.* Practice the conversation again. Use the excuses on page 94.

ROLE PLAY

1. *Pairs.* Make plans with your partner to do something next week. For example, Let's go out for coffee next Thursday after class.

2. Find three classmates to join you.

   Ⓐ We're going out for coffee/to a movie/to my house/dancing/out to dinner/ to a party next Thursday after class. Do you want to come?
   Ⓑ I'd love to.
   Ⓒ I'd love to, but I can't. I have to...

3. Report to the class. For example, Terry, Walt, Monica, and I are going out for coffee after class next Thursday. Sue can't come. She has to study.

GRAMMAR

Do you **like sushi?**	I love it. Yeah, it's OK. Not really. I hate it.	Do you **like to dance?**	I love to. Yeah. Not really. I hate to.

CONVERSATION

1. Practice the conversations.

2. *Pairs.* Practice the conversations again. Use the cues.

FIND SOMEONE

1. Write your favorite food, singer/group, TV show, and activity:

Food	Singer/Group	TV show	Activity

   Find someone who likes the same things as you. Use *Do you like...?*
   or *Do you like to...?*

2. Report to the class. For example, *Matt and I love french fries. Stephie and
   I really like....*

TIC-TAC-TOE

Pairs. Student A is X. Student B is O. Take turns.

- Student A, choose a square.
- Make a sentence with the verb in the square. For example, *I like pizza.*
- If the sentence is correct, put your X on the square. If the sentence is not
  correct, do not put an X on the square.
- Student B, take your turn.
- The winner is the first one to get 3 Xs or 3 Os in a line →, ↓, or ↘.

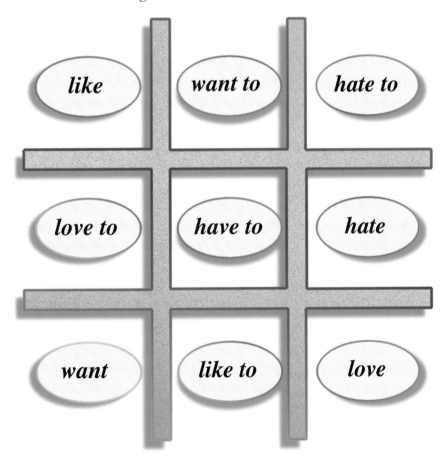

READING AND WRITING

1. Skim the letters and circle the correct answer.

Terry is an expert in:

    a. letter writing   **b.** good manners   **c.** computers

The letters are:

    a. on a computer network   **b.** on a TV show   **c.** in a newspaper

---

ETIQUETTE NET—ASK TERRY
<tips@goodmanners.com>

From: Rick<"rick@ubv.buffalo.edu">
TO: ASK TERRY <"tips@goodmanners.com">
Subject: Dinner Gift

>Dear Terry,
>I'm a first-year student in college and I'm living in a dorm. The parents of one of
>my classmates invited me to their house for dinner next week. Should I take
>something? If so, what? — Rick

Dear Rick,
Yes, you should definitely take something when someone invites you to dinner. You
can take a box of chocolates or some flowers. By the way, if you get flowers, don't
get them in a vase! Of course, as soon as you are 21, you can also take some wine.
Plan to spend about $10. — Terry

- -

From: Irena <"irena@uwashington.edu">
TO: ASK TERRY <"tips@goodmanners.com">
Subject: Dinner Time

>Dear Terry,
>I'm from another country. I'm going to a dinner party on Thursday night. The
>invitation says 7:00 p.m. What time should I arrive? — Irena

Dear Irena,
If the invitation says seven o'clock, arrive at seven o'clock sharp. In the U.S., you have
to be on time to a dinner party. It's rude to arrive late. However, for regular parties
you can arrive up to an hour late. — Terry

- -

From: Dave <"dave@stanford.edu">
TO: ASK TERRY <"tips@goodmanners.com">
Subject: Party Guests

>Dear Terry,
>This morning some old friends called and said they were coming to town
>tomorrow night. They're going to stay with me for a couple of days. Here is the
>problem: I'm invited to a party tomorrow night, and I really want to go. Can I take
>my friends? — Dave

Dear Dave,
If you're invited to a dinner party, you cannot take your friends. If it's just a regular
party and only two or three friends are coming to visit you, call your host NOW and
ask if it's OK to bring a few people with you. — Terry

2. Look at the pictures. Cross out the ones that illustrate bad manners.

September 4

Dear Marty,
Bill and I are having a small
dinner party for Marion on Friday,
September 22, at 7:30 p.m.
It's her birthday. We hope you can come.

a.

Can I bring a couple of friends to your party tonight?

b.

c.

Hi, Steve. I brought a few friends. I hope it's OK.

d.

We're having a _Valentine's Day dinner_ party
Date: _Saturday, February 14_
Time: _7 p.m._
Place: _607 Elm Street_
Bring a friend!

e.

f.

3. *Pairs.* Check your answers. Say why the pictures show good or bad manners.

> Ⓐ Picture "a" shows bad manners because….
> Ⓑ Right. And picture "b"….

4. Choose one of the letters to Terry. Write an answer according to customs in your country.

5. *Pairs.* Share your answers.

WORLD VIEW

Bad manners vary from country to country.

Korea: You should never blow your nose in front of people.
United States: You should never slurp or burp while eating.
Japan: You should never pour your own drink.

What are some bad manners in your country?

What's the matter?

VOCABULARY

1. Listen to the conversations. Write the reason under each picture.

Steve, angry
<u>Someone took his wallet.</u>

Sally, excited

_____

Roberta, worried

_____

Andy, nervous

_____

Dan, embarrassed

_____

Alice, happy

_____

Kevin, annoyed

_____

Barbara, disappointed

_____

Ben, upset

_____

2. _Pairs._ Check your answers.

Ⓐ Why is Steve angry?
Ⓑ Because someone took his wallet. Why is Sally excited?

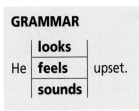

GRAMMAR

He	looks	upset.
	feels	
	sounds	

CONVERSATION

1. Practice the conversation.

Becky: Hi, Brett.
Brett: Oh, hi, Becky.
Becky: You look **upset.**
What's going on?
Brett: I just found out that my best friend is moving to Canada.
Becky: Oh, that's too bad.

2. *Pairs.* Practice the conversation again. Use the information on page 100.
Use *That's too bad* or *That's great.*

Personalize

3. *Pairs.* Practice the conversation again. Use your own information.

LISTENING

1. Listen. How does each speaker feel? Circle the correct word.

Speaker 1	happy	nervous	annoyed
Speaker 2	upset	excited	disappointed
Speaker 3	excited	worried	angry
Speaker 4	angry	worried	happy

2. *Pairs.* Check your answers.

Ⓐ Speaker 1 sounds happy.
Ⓑ Right. And Speaker 2 sounds....

CONVERSATION

1. Practice the conversation.

> Dan: What's wrong, **Pat?** You don't look very happy.
> Pat: I'm not. I'm really nervous. **I have a job interview** later.
> Dan: Oh, yeah?
> Pat: Uh-huh. I always get nervous when **I have a job interview.**
> Dan: Yeah, I know what you mean.

2. *Pairs.* Practice the conversation again. Use the cues.

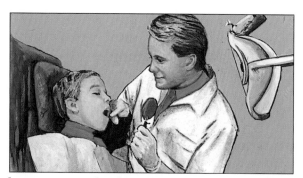

have a test

have a blind date

have to go to the dentist

have to give a speech

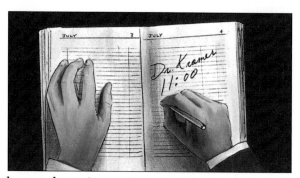

have a doctor's appointment

have to take a plane trip

PRONUNCIATION

1. Listen. Notice the intonation and phrasing of the following sentences.

I always get angry when people litter.

I always get annoyed when people smoke in my office.

I always get nervous when I have to give a speech.

2. Listen to these sentences said three times. Which one has the correct intonation and phrasing? Circle 1, 2, or 3.

   a. I'm always embarrassed when I'm late for a meeting. 1 2 3

   b. I'm always happy when the weather is nice. 1 2 3

   c. I'm always disappointed when people forget my birthday. 1 2 3

3. Now say the sentences in Exercises 1 and 2.

MAKE IT PERSONAL

1. Copy the chart on a separate piece of paper. Interview three classmates. Begin, *When do you get embarrassed?*

Classmate's Name	embarrassed	angry	nervous
Abraham	when the teacher asks him a question and he can't answer		

2. Report to the class. For example, *Abraham gets embarrassed when the teacher asks him a question and he can't answer.*

READING AND WRITING

1. *Pairs.* Look at the list of phobias (fears). Which do you think are the three most common phobias?

FEAR OF

water—hydrophobia
heights—acrophobia
lightning—astraphobia
social situations—sociophobia
spiders—arachnophobia

insects—entomophobia
flying—aerophobia
open spaces—agoraphobia
closed spaces—claustrophobia
death—necrophobia

2. Read the article. Choose the best title.

a. Phobias   **b.** Fear of Flying   **c.** Karen's Problem

"It's awful. I can't breathe. My heart goes a mile a minute. My stomach gets upset. I feel dizzy, and I think I'm going to faint." What do you think Karen Daniels is talking about? Having brain surgery? Skydiving? No. She's talking about getting on a plane!

Karen is one of millions of people who have aerophobia, fear of flying. For ten years, Karen didn't fly because she was so afraid. Every time she thought about flying, she panicked.

Of course, it's natural to fear flying. In fact, many people with aerophobia are reasonable and intelligent. They just can't believe that tons of aluminum and steel will stay up in the sky.

Yet there are ways to overcome aerophobia. First, people need to face the fear and then take steps to relieve it. Some of these steps are listed in this article. There are also many courses to help all those executives, college students, and other reasonable people overcome their fear of flying.

What can you do?

► Do deep-breathing and relaxation exercises before you get on the plane.

► Picture the airplane landing safely.

► Don't have caffeine. (Beverages such as coffee, tea, and colas, and foods with chocolate all contain caffeine.)

► When you're on a plane, don't just sit still—stretch you arms and legs.

► Learn how planes fly.

► Take a course for overcoming the fear of flying.

3. Every paragraph has a main idea. What's the main idea of each paragraph in the article?

Paragraph 1

Karen Daniels is talking about getting on a plane.

Paragraph 2

Paragraph 3

Paragraph 4

4. Imagine that one of your friends has a phobia. Write him or her a letter giving advice. For example, your friend is afraid of heights, afraid of the dark, afraid of elevators, or afraid to speak English.

5. *Pairs.* Read your letter to your partner. Don't mention the phobia. Your partner should guess what the phobia is.

Word roots and common phobias

Phobia is from a Greek root word meaning *fear.* According to Russel Ash in *The Top Ten of Everything,* the three most common phobias are arachnophobia, sociophobia, and aerophobia.

Did you guess correctly?

16 Whatever will be, will be!

LISTENING

1. Listen to the predictions for the year 2025. Write *A* for Amy's predictions and *B* for Bob's predictions.

— There won't be enough food.

— We won't have any more wars.

— It will be hotter.

— It won't rain enough.

— We'll know how to grow food in the ocean.

2025

B There will be 10 billion people in the world.

— There won't be any more rain forests.

— There will be a cure for cancer.

— People won't waste water.

— People will live in space.

2. *Pairs.* Check your answers.

    (A) Bob thinks there'll be 10 billion people in the world.
    (B) Right. And Amy thinks…

3. Who's the optimist, Amy or Bob? Who's the pessimist?

Personalize

4. *Pairs.* What do you think? Use the predictions on page 106.

    (A) I think there'll be 10 billion people in the world.
    (B) I don't think so. I think…

WORLD VIEW

Optimistic and pessimistic countries

Nations can also be optimists or pessimists. One poll found that people in Venezuela and Germany were most pessimistic about the future. People were most optimistic in Taiwan, India, and Thailand.

Are people in your country generally optimistic or pessimistic?

THINK FAST

1. *Groups.* You have ten minutes. Brainstorm as many predictions for the year 2025 as you can. One person writes the ideas. The group with the most predictions wins.

2. Report to the class. For example, *Our group thinks there won't be any more pollution.*

CONVERSATION

Practice the conversation.

Bob: You're such an optimist, Amy! What do you think you'll be doing in 2025?

Amy: Oh, I think I'll be a famous artist. And, let's see, I'll have an apartment in Paris and I'll have my own gallery. And, of course, I'll be happily married. And I'll have two beautiful children. What about you?

PRONUNCIATION

1. Listen. Notice the pronunciation of the contractions with *will*.

She'll be a doctor in five years.

They'll go to Rome next year.

We'll probably have three children by the year 2030.

He'll call tomorrow.

You'll feel better soon.

I'll see you later.

2. Listen. Fill in the blanks.

1. _____He'll_____ get a new job next year.

2. _____ have factories on Mars in the year 2050.

3. _____ be rich and famous in five years.

4. _____ speak five languages by the year 2040.

3. Now say the sentences in Exercises 1 and 2.

LISTENING

1. Listen to the rest of the conversation. Write three more sentences about Bob's life in the future.

   He'll be a doctor.

   _____

   _____

   _____

2. *Pairs.* Check your answers.

   Ⓐ In 2025, Bob will be a doctor.
   Ⓑ Right. And he'll…

When I grow up I'll be an old woman.

WHAT WILL THEY BE DOING?

Pairs.
Go to page 130.

MAKE IT PERSONAL

1. *Pairs.* Take turns. Ask your partner what he or she will be doing in five years. Take notes.

   Ⓐ What do you think you'll be doing in five years?
   Ⓑ I'll be a successful accountant.

2. Report to the class. For example, *In five years, Martha will be a successful accountant. She'll….*

READING AND WRITING

1. *Pairs.* Cover the article. How do you think we will pay for things in the year 2025? Brainstorm.

2. Read the article. Does it have any of your ideas from Exercise 1?

PAYING FOR IT IN THE FUTURE

Do you hate to carry money around? Do you get holes in your pockets from heavy coins? Well, just wait. By the year 2025, you won't need money at all. Here are some ways you'll be paying for things in the future.

There will probably still be credit cards, but most businesses will have fingerprint machines. To pay for things you'll just put your fingers on the machine. The machine will then send an electronic message to your bank, and the bank will transfer the money from your account to the business's account.

Another quick and easy way to pay will be by using a computer in a video camera. You'll just go to a store, pick up the items you want, and leave. As you leave the store, a video camera will record you. A computer inside the camera will scan your image and the price tag of your items. It will then bill your credit card or bank account automatically.

Some people think we won't need money or credit cards by the year 2025 because there won't be any stores by then. They think we'll do all our shopping through computers or interactive TV. It will be possible to see all items — clothing, food, tools, electronic devices, jewelry, cars, appliances, etc. — on the TV screen. You'll just have to say the name of the item or touch the picture on the screen and that item will arrive at your door in a few hours.

You'll never have to touch money or plastic cards. The whole transaction will be electronic.

JACK WARD
442-095-7787
COTTON PANTS: $45.92

1 quart milk	$2.00
2 lb. apples	$4.75
Blouse	$25.60
Car radio	$195.23
Tax	$27.50
Total	$255.08

Eggs	$2.33
1 quart milk	$2.00
Butter	$4.88
Half pint cream	$3.20
Margarine	$2.77

A dozen eggs and a pound of butter.

3. Vocabulary in context. Find the following words in the article. Re-read the paragraph and guess the meaning of the word from context.

holes	fingerprint	electronic	transfer	account
record	image	price tag	bill	items
screen	touch	plastic	transaction	

4. The article talks about three ways we will pay for things in the future. What are they?

_____ _____ _____

5. *Pairs.* Discuss. Do you think the ways we will pay for things in the future are good? Why or why not? For example, *I think the ways we will pay for things will/will not be good because…*

6. Write an essay about either technology or travel in the year 2025. Use these pictures for ideas.

   a. First, do a freewriting on the topic. (Freewriting helps you get ideas for writing. Write for five minutes. DON'T STOP. An example of freewriting for this article is on page 130.)

   b. Use the ideas from your freewriting to write a first draft of your essay. Write at least three paragraphs.

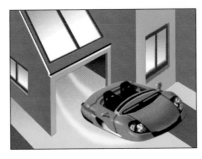
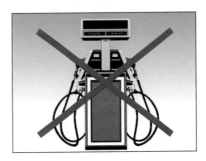

7. *Pairs.* Share your essays.

Strategy Session Four

LISTENING

Strategy: Using your knowledge of grammar

🔊 1. Listen to the news report. It's about something in the …

    a. past   **b.** present   **c.** future

🔊 2. Listen again. Write three phrases that helped you decide.

    _____

    _____

    _____

Strategy: Listening for specific information

🔊 3. Listen to the news report again. Answer the questions.

    In what city will the MTV Music Awards ceremony be? _____

    In what theater? _____

    On what day and date? _____

    How many tickets will be on sale? _____

    Who will be there? _____

    When will the tickets go on sale? _____

    Where will the tickets go on sale? _____

    How many tickets can one person buy? _____

    How much are the tickets? _____

4. *Pairs.* Check your answers.

    Ⓐ The MTV Music Awards will be in….

VOCABULARY LEARNING

Strategy: Forming mental images

For example:

1. Look through Units 13–16. Find six words you want to remember by forming mental images.

2. *Pairs.* Student A, draw or describe your mental image. Student B, guess the word.

Strategy: Testing yourself

1. Look at the picture. Think of as many words as you can in English. Say the words softly to yourself.

2. *Pairs.* Take turns telling each other the words you remembered.

3. Look around as you go home. How many things can you name in English?

CONVERSATION MANAGEMENT

Strategy: Using hesitaters

🔊 1. Listen to the conversation and fill in the blanks with these hesitaters:

    oh   *uh*   *let's see*   *hmm*   *you know*   *well*

A: Did you see that new miniseries last night?

B: I sure did. It was great!

A: What do you think will happen tonight?

B: _Hmm_. _____, I think Emma will leave Tom for that doctor, _____, Paul.

A: Really?

B: Of course. And then, _____, Tom will get very sick and have to go to the hospital.

A: Right! And, _____, Paul will be his doctor and he'll have to do open heart surgery on Tom.

B: Right. Right. And, _____, Paul will save Tom's life.

A: Yes! And, Emma will realize that she loves Tom and they will live happily ever after!

2. *Pairs.* Check your answers. Then role-play the conversation.

3. *Pairs.* Student A, make predictions about a TV series or soap opera, OR talk about your city or country in the year 2015. Use hesitaters when you need them. Student B, keep the conversation going. Comment and ask questions.

GRAMMAR LEARNING

Strategy: Reviewing

Slides and Ladders

Pairs. Use one book.

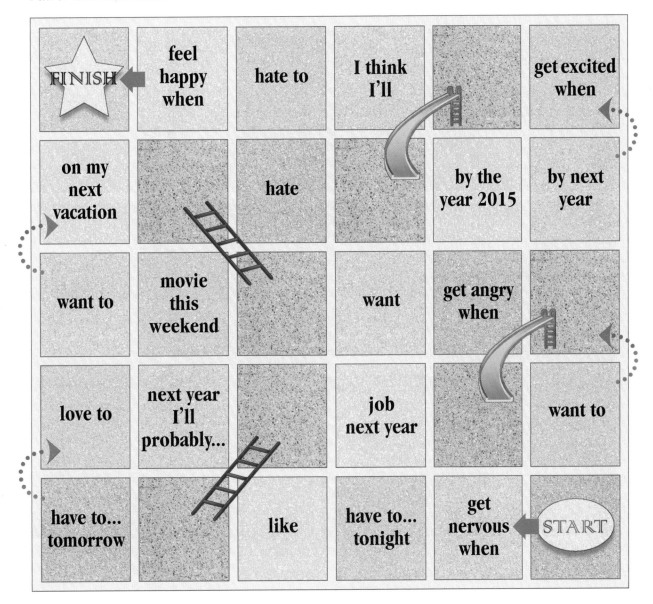

- Each student, put a marker on Start.
- Student A, flip a coin. Heads = 1; tails = 2. Move your marker one or two squares.
- If you land on a square with some words, make a true sentence about yourself with the words. For example, A: *I get nervous when I go to the doctor.*

- If your sentence is wrong, move back one square.
- If you land on a square with a slide, you go down. If you land on a square with a ladder, you go up.
- The first one to get to Finish is the winner.

Strategy: Analyzing your grammar errors   Go to page 123.

Unit 1: Your own game show

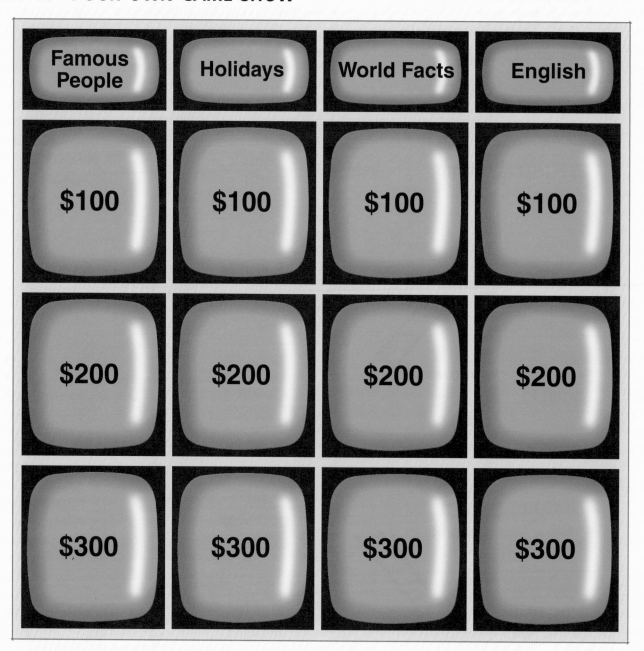

- Choose a category and amount. For example, *Holidays for $100.*
- Listen to Pair 1's question and answer it.
- If your answer is correct, circle the amount. $100
- If your answer is not correct, put an X over the amount. $100
- After you have answered all 12 questions, total your winnings.
- Then go to page 5, switch roles, and play the game again.

UNIT 2: BINGO

1. Choose one card.

2. Listen to the descriptions. For example, you may hear *She has long red hair and green eyes*. If you have the person described on your card, cover the picture. The winner is the first one to cover three pictures in a line:
→, ↓, or ↘.

UNIT 7: WHAT DID SHE DO LAST MONDAY?

Student A

1. Tell Student B about Linda.

   A: Last Monday night, Linda cleaned house. Last Tuesday night, she....

2. Listen to Student B. Write the things Katy did.

WEEKLY PLANNER				
MONDAY	TUESDAY	WEDNESDAY	THURSDAY	FRIDAY
She visited friends.				
Katy	SATURDAY		SUNDAY	

3. *Pairs.* Look at Rick's schedule on page 131. Is he Linda's or Katy's boyfriend? How do you know? Begin: *I think Rick is ___'s boyfriend because they both....*

UNIT 4: WHOSE IS WHOSE?

Student A

1. You have a picture of Liza's apartment. Make a list of her living room and bedroom furniture and her kitchen furniture and appliances.

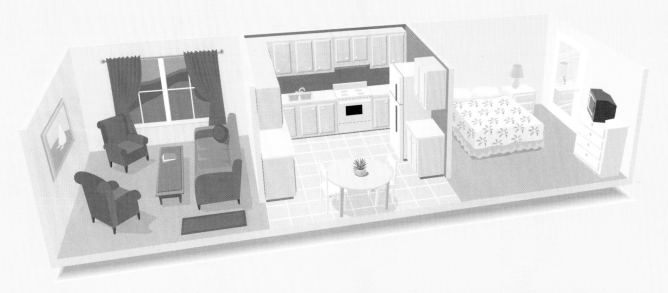

2. Student B has a picture of Don's apartment. The apartment is the same as Liza's, but the furniture is different. Take turns asking about the furniture in the pictures. Take notes.

Ⓐ There's a blue couch in Liza's living room. Is there a couch in Don's?

Ⓑ Yes, there is, but it's green. There's a...

Liza's Apartment	Don's Apartment
Living room	
a blue couch	
Bedroom	
Kitchen	

Unit 4: Whose is whose?

Student B

1. You have a picture of Don's apartment. Make a list of his living room and bedroom furniture and his kitchen furniture and appliances.

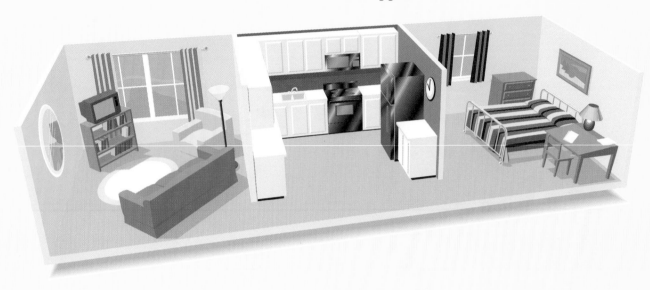

2. Student A has a picture of Liza's apartment. The apartment is the same as Don's, but the furniture is different. Take turns asking about the furniture in the pictures. Take notes.

Ⓐ There's a blue couch in Liza's living room. Is there a couch in Don's?

Ⓑ Yes, there is, but it's green. There's a…

Don's Apartment	Liza's Apartment
Living room	
a green couch	
Bedroom	
Kitchen	

STRATEGY SESSION ONE: GRAMMAR LEARNING

Strategy: Noticing language patterns

	to be, present	simple present
Affirmative Statements	He's tall.	He has dark hair.
Negative Statements	He's not tall.	He doesn't have dark hair.
Yes/No Questions	Is he tall?	Does he have dark hair?
Information Questions	How tall is he?	What color hair does he have?

1. Look at the examples of each pattern above. Then fill in the blanks below.

Affirmative Statements	I'm 21 years old.	I work from 9:00 to 5:00.
Negative Statements	_____	_____
Yes/No Questions	____ you ____ ?	____ you ____ ?
Information Questions	____ you ____ ?	____ you ____ ?
Affirmative Statements	They're in Egypt.	They speak Spanish.
Negative Statements	_____	_____
Yes/No Questions	_____ ?	_____ ?
Information Questions	_____ ?	_____

2. Pairs. Check your answers with a partner's.

STRATEGY SESSION TWO: GRAMMAR LEARNING

Strategy: Classifying

1. Write the past tense of these verbs:

marry	_____	listen	_____
take	_____	sleep	_____
is	_____	miss	_____
read	_____	eat	_____

2. The past tense of verbs can be regular or irregular. Regular verbs end in *-ed*. Classify the verbs in Exercise 1. Then check your answers with a partner.

   Regular verbs:

   Irregular verbs:

3. Look through Units 5–8. Choose ten verbs. Classify them on a separate piece of paper. Then check your answers with a partner.

UNIT 7: WHAT DID SHE DO LAST MONDAY?

Student B

1. Listen to Student A. Write the things Linda did.

MONDAY	TUESDAY	WEDNESDAY	THURSDAY	FRIDAY
She cleaned house.				

Linda

	SATURDAY		SUNDAY	

2. Tell Student A about Katy.

B: Last Monday night, Katy visited friends. Last Tuesday night, she....

3. *Pairs.* Look at Rick's schedule on page 131. Is he Linda's or Katy's boyfriend? How do you know? Begin: *I think Rick is ____'s boyfriend because they both....*

STRATEGY SESSION THREE: GRAMMAR LEARNING

Strategy: Keeping a grammar journal

A grammar journal is a record of your errors in English grammar. You will use this journal in Strategy Session Four to learn from your mistakes.

As you study the last four units of this book, keep a list of all the errors you make in class and in your homework. Write the mistakes in your journal and correct them. Use a separate piece of paper. For example,

Grammar Journal

Error	Correction
I studying English.	I'm studying English.

STRATEGY SESSION FOUR: GRAMMAR LEARNING

Strategy: Analyzing your grammar errors

1. Sometimes it helps to look at errors to see patterns. What patterns do you see in these examples?

Error	Correction
I studying English.	I'm studying English.
We going to the park.	We're going to the park.
I love to, but I can't.	I'd love to, but I can't.
I always get nervous when I had a job interview.	I always get nervous when I have a job interview.

2. Look at your grammar journal. Do you see any patterns in your errors?

3. *Pairs.* Tell your partner about your errors. For example, *I leave out the verb "to be" when I use the present continuous tense.*

UNIT 9: WHERE'S THE SOAP?

Student B

1. Imagine that you and Student A are sharing a hotel room. Put these things in your room. (Write the words in the picture.)

   razors   shoe cloth   conditioner   bottled water   soap

2. Answer Student A's questions about where the things are.

   Ⓐ Where did you put the razors?
   Ⓑ They're….

3. You can't find these things. Ask Student A where they are. Write the words in the correct place in the picture.

   shaving cream   toothpaste   hand lotion   shampoo   robes

Unit 12: Where is she going?

Student A

1. Look at the pictures. Cindy is going to the island of Maui. Tell Student B what she is going to do there. Student B has to guess which island Cindy is going to. Begin: *Cindy is going to fly to one of the islands. She's going to go to....*

2. Now ask Student B, *Which island is she going to go to?*

3. Listen to Student B. Look at the pictures. Which island are Dan and Esther going to?

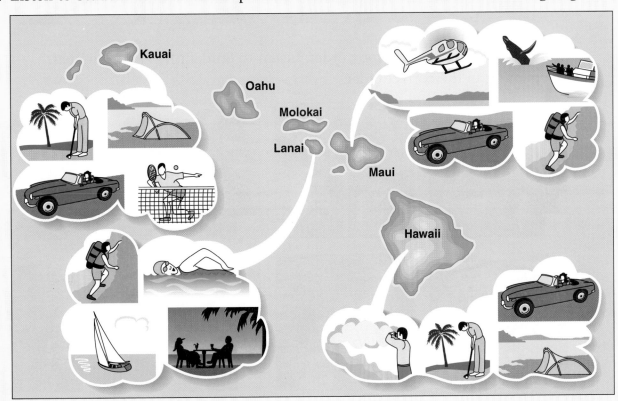

UNIT 10: WHAT'S THE STORY?

Student A

1. Look at the pictures. Tell
Student B the story. What are
Mike, Carol, and Sherry doing
in each picture? Student B has
to number the pictures in the
correct order.

Mike

Carol

Sherry

2. You have pictures in the wrong order. Listen to Student B's story. Number
the pictures in the correct order.

3. Finish the story. Decide together. What's happening now?

Unit 9: Where's the soap?

Student A

1. Imagine that you and Student B are sharing a hotel room. Put these things in your room. (Write the words in the picture.)

   shaving cream   toothpaste   hand lotion   shampoo   robes

2. You can't find these things. Ask Student B where they are. Write the words in the correct place in the picture.

   razors   shoe cloth   conditioner   bottled water   soap

   (A) Where did you put the razors?
   (B) They're....

3. Answer Student B's questions about where the things are.

UNIT 12 WHERE IS SHE GOING?

Student B

1. Listen to Student A. Look at the pictures. Which island is Cindy going to go to?

2. Look at the pictures. Dan and Esther are going to fly to the island of Hawaii. Tell Student A what they are going to do there. Student A has to guess which island Dan and Esther are going to. Begin: *Dan and Esther are going to fly to one of the islands. They're going to....*

3. Now ask Student A, *Which island are they going to go to?*

UNIT 10: WHAT'S THE STORY?

Student B

1. You have pictures in the wrong order. Listen to Student A's story. Number the pictures in the correct order.

Mike

Carol

Sherry

2. Look at the pictures. Tell Student A the story. What are Mike, Carol, and Sherry doing in each picture? Student A has to number the pictures in the correct order.

3. Finish the story. Decide together. What's happening now?

UNIT 16: WHAT WILL THEY BE DOING?

Pairs. Matt Dart and Donna Simms will be married next week. What will they be doing in ten years? Look at the picture and make as many sentences as you can about their future. For example, *They'll have an apartment in the city.* The pair with the most sentences wins.

UNIT 16: FREEWRITING EXAMPLE

In the future instead of using money we will probably use credit cards. There will be machines everywhere and we will be able to buy little things like newspapers, magazines, candy, soda, etc., with credit cards. No one will have to carry money. Let's see—what else can I say—Oh, maybe fingerprints. Stores will have machines that can read fingerprints.

UNIT 7

Rick's Schedule

UNIT 10

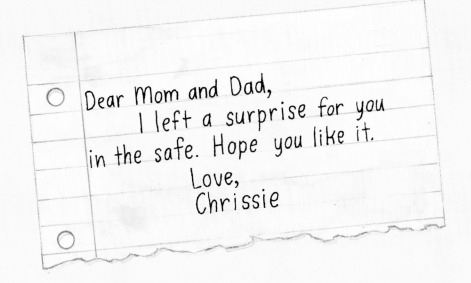

UNIT 4

Grammar Summary

PRESENT TENSE OF BE

Affirmative Statements

FULL FORM			CONTRACTION
I	am	→	I'm
You	are	→	You're
He	is	→	He's
She	is	→	She's
It	is	→	It's
We	are	→	We're
They	are	→	They're

Negative Statements

FULL FORM			CONTRACTION
I	am not	→	I'm not
You	are not	→	You aren't/You're not
He	is not	→	He isn't/He's not
She	is not	→	She isn't/She's not
It	is not	→	It isn't/It's not
We	are not	→	We aren't/We're not
They	are not	→	They aren't/They're not

Yes/No Questions

Am	I	
Are	you	
Is	he	
Is	she	there?
Is	it	
Are	we	
Are	they	

Short Answers

	I	am.			I	'm not.
	you	are.			you	aren't.
	he	is.			he	isn't.
Yes,	she	is.		No,	she	isn't.
	it	is.			it	isn't.
	we	are.			we	aren't.
	they	are.			they	aren't.

Information Questions

	am	I?
	are	you?
	is	he?
Where	is	she?
	is	it?
	are	we?
	are	they?

SIMPLE PRESENT TENSE

Affirmative Statements

I	work.
You	work.
He	works.
She	works.
It	works.
We	work.
They	work.

Negative Statements

I	don't	
You	don't	
He	doesn't	
She	doesn't	work.
It	doesn't	
We	don't	
They	don't	

Information Questions

	do	I	
	do	you	
	does	he	
Where	does	she	work?
	does	it	
	do	we	
	do	they	

Yes/No Questions

Do	I	
Do	you	
Does	he	
Does	she	work?
Does	it	
Do	we	
Do	they	

Short Answers

	I	do.			I	don't.
	you	do.			you	don't.
	he	does.			he	doesn't.
Yes,	she	does.		No,	she	doesn't.
	it	does.			it	doesn't.
	we	do.			we	don't.
	they	do.			they	don't.

THERE IS/THERE ARE

Affirmative Statements

There	is	a hotel	near here.
	are	two hotels	

Negative Statements

There	isn't	a hotel	near here.
	aren't	any hotels	

Yes/No Questions

Is there	a hotel	near here?
Are there	any hotels	

Short Answers

Yes,	there is.	No,	there isn't.
	there are.		there aren't.

SIMPLE PAST TENSE OF BE

Affirmative Statements

I	was	
You	were	
He	was	
She	was	there.
It	was	
We	were	
They	were	

Negative Statements

I	was not	(wasn't)	
You	were not	(weren't)	
He	was not	(wasn't)	
She	was not	(wasn't)	there.
It	was not	(wasn't)	
We	were not	(weren't)	
They	were not	(weren't)	

Information Questions

	was	I	
	were	you	
How often	was	he	
When	was	she	there?
Why	was	it	
	were	we	
	were	they	

Yes/No Questions

Was	I	
Were	you	
Was	he	
Was	she	there?
Was	it	
Were	we	
Were	they	

Short Answers

Yes,	I	was.	No,	I	wasn't.
	you	were.		you	weren't.
	he	was.		he	wasn't.
	she	was.		she	wasn't.
	it	was.		it	wasn't.
	we	were.		we	weren't.
	they	were.		they	weren't.

SIMPLE PAST TENSE

Affirmative Statements

I	worked.
You	worked.
He	worked.
She	worked.
It	worked.
We	worked.
They	worked.

Negative Statements

I	didn't	work.
You	didn't	work.
He	didn't	work.
She	didn't	work.
It	didn't	work.
We	didn't	work.
They	didn't	work.

Information Questions

	did	I	
	did	you	
Where	did	he	
When	did	she	work?
How often	did	it	
	did	we	
	did	they	

Yes/No questions

Did	I	
Did	you	
Did	he	
Did	she	work?
Did	it	
Did	we	
Did	they	

Short Answers

Yes,	I	did.	No,	I	didn't.
	you	did.		you	didn't.
	he	did.		he	didn't.
	she	did.		she	didn't.
	it	did.		it	didn't.
	we	did.		we	didn't.
	they	did.		they	didn't.

PRESENT PROGRESSIVE

Affirmative Statements		Negative Statements		Information Questions		
I	am ('m)	I	am ('m) not		am	I
You	are ('re)	You	are ('re) not		are	you
He	is ('s)	He	is ('s) not	Where	is	he
She	is ('s) working.	She	is ('s) not working.	How	is	she working?
It	is ('s)	It	is ('s) not		is	it
We	are ('re)	We	are ('re) not		are	we
They	are ('re)	They	are ('re) not		are	they

Yes/No questions		Short Answers				
Am	I		I	am.		I	'm not.
Are	you		you	are.		you	aren't.
Is	he		he	is.		he	isn't.
Is	she working?	Yes,	she	is.	No,	she	isn't.
Is	it		it	is.		it	isn't.
Are	we		we	are.		we	aren't.
Are	they		they	are.		they	aren't.

FUTURE TENSE WITH GOING TO

Affirmative Statements		Negative Statements		Information Questions		
I	am ('m)	I	am ('m)		am	I
You	are ('re)	You	are ('re)		are	you
He	is ('s)	He	is ('s)	Where	is	he
She	is ('s) going to work.	She	is ('s) going to work.	When	is	she going to work?
It	is ('s)	It	is ('s)	How	is	it
We	are ('re)	We	are ('re)		are	we
They	are ('re)	They	are ('re)		are	they

Yes/No questions		Short Answers				
I	am ('m)		I	am.		I	'm not.
You	are ('re)		you	are.		you	aren't.
He	is ('s)		he	is.		he	isn't.
She	is ('s) going to work.	Yes,	she	is.	No,	she	isn't.
It	is ('s)		it	is.		it	isn't.
We	are ('re)		we	are.		we	aren't.
They	are ('re)		they	are.		they	aren't.

FUTURE TENSE WITH WILL

Affirmative Statements			Negative Statements			Information Questions			
I	will ('ll)		I	will not (won't)			will	I	
You	will ('ll)		You	will not (won't)			will	you	
He	will ('ll)		He	will not (won't)		When	will	he	
She	will ('ll)	move.	She	will not (won't)	move.	How	will	she	move?
It	will ('ll)		It	will not (won't)			will	it	
We	will ('ll)		We	will not (won't)			will	we	
They	will ('ll)		They	will not (won't)			will	they	

Yes/No questions			Short Answers					
	I			I	will.		I	won't.
	you			you	will.		you	won't.
	he			he	will.		we	won't.
Will	she	move?	Yes,	she	will.	No,	they	won't.
	it			it	will.		he	won't.
	we			we	will.		she	won't.
	they			they	will.		it	won't.

DEMONSTRATIVE ADJECTIVES

For things near the speaker:

What's this?
What are these?

For things far from the speaker:

What's that?
What are those?

POSSESSIVES

Possessive adjectives				's
		my		Kate's glasses
		your		Charles's keys
		his		
This	is	her	test	
		its		
		our		
		their		

ADVERBS OF FREQUENCY

How often do you read the newspaper?

I	always	read	the newspaper.
	usually		
	often		
	sometimes		
	never		

I	read the newspaper	once a week.
		twice a week.
		three times a week.

ADVERB CLAUSES (WHEN)

I get nervous | when I have a test.   or   When I have a test, | I get nervous.

PREPOSITIONS OF LOCATION

	next to	the shirts.
	across from	the elevator.
Where is it? It's	between	the shoes and the gloves.
	on	Highway 66.
	on the corner of	Aspen Avenue and Agassiz Street.

	on	the counter.
	in	the drawer.
It's	over	the sink.
	under	the sink.
	in the corner	the room.

ARTICLES

Indefinite (a/an)

a dentist (use a before consonant sounds)

an accountant (use an before vowel sounds)

actors (use no indefinite article before plurals)

Definite (the)

the dentist (use the for a specific person, place, or thing)

COUNT/NONCOUNT NOUNS

Yes/No Questions

	an	iron?
Could I have	some	toothpaste?
	some	towels?

Answers

	one.
Yes, we'll give you	some.

	one.
No, we don't have	any.

PRONOUNS

Personal Pronouns

I
You
He
She
It
We
They

Object Pronouns

	me.
	you.
	her.
He saw	him.
	it.
	them.
	us.

Possessive Pronouns

		mine.
		yours
		his.
Whose house is it?	It's	hers.
		its.
		ours.
		theirs.

Reflexive Pronouns

I		myself.
You		yourself.
He		himself.
She	washed	herself.
It		itself.
We		ourself.
They		themselves.